MEN UNDER CONSTRUCTION

MEN UNDER CONSTRUCTION

DONALD JOY

Revised, Expanded Edition of the Book
Formerly Titled *Un-finished Business.*

VICTOR BOOKS

A DIVISION OF SCRIPTURE PRESS PUBLICATIONS INC.
USA CANADA ENGLAND

Unless otherwise noted, all Scripture quotations are from the *Holy Bible, New International Version®*. Copyright © 1973, 1978, 1984 by International Bible Society. Used by permission of Zondervan Publishing House. All rights reserved. Other quotations are taken from the *Authorized (King James) Version* (KJV); and from *The New English Bible* (NEB), © 1961, 1970, Oxford and Cambridge University Press.

Editor: Greg D. Clouse
Designer: Scott Rattray
Cover Illustrator: Marilyn King

Library of Congress Cataloging-in-Publication Data

Joy, Donald M. (Donald Marvin), 1928–
   Men under construction / by Donald M. Joy
     p.   cm.
   Rev. ed. of: Unfinished business. 1989.
   Includes bibliographical references and index.
   ISBN 1-56476-053-7
   1. Masculinity (Psychology) 2. Men – Psychology.
   3. Men – Religious life. 4. Christian life – 1960– I. Joy, Donald M.
(Donald Marvin), 1928– Unfinished business. II. Title.
  BF692.5.J69 1993
  155.6'32 – dc20   92-42714
                                              CIP

---

1 2 3 4 5 6 7 8 9 10 Printing/Year 97 96 95 94 93

OTHER BOOKS IN THIS SERIES

CONTENTS

DEDICATION

To the Men Who Joined Me Under Construction 1972-1992

Craig Adams
Tony Akers
Carey Akin
Terry Alderson
Jim Allen
Rick Alnutt
David Anderson
Doug Anderson
Ken Argot
David Ashworth
Joe Aurand
John Baird
Brent Baker
David Ballinger
Carey Balzer
Med Barr
Sam Bartlett
David Barton
John Bartz
Bob Beebe
Ben Belcher
Pat Bennett
Randy Bennett
Steve Benson
Greg Bentle
Tim Berger
Bill Bergstrom
Dennis Blackwell
Paul Blair
Steve Blakemore
Bryan Blankenship
David Blincoe
Steve Boom
Bart Bowlin
Dan Boyd
Tim Bracken
Carl Brannon
Don Bridges
Philip Bridgewater
John Britt
Bob Brothers
Scott Brown
David Brownlee
Ed Bryson
David Buckner
Kent Byer
Bobby Cain
Mark Cain
David Carey
Russ Carter
Walter Carter
Shelley Caulder
Rick Charles
Craig Cheney
Mike Childs
Kurt Church
Glen Clark
J.P. Clark

Jay Clark
Rick Clyde
Gary Coates
Gerry Coates
Jerry Coleman
Jack Connell
David Cotton
Keith Cowart
Kevin Crawford
Doug Cross
Mark Cross
Jay Crouse
Todd Danningburg
Casey Davis
Jerry Davis
Wesley Davis
Steve Dawson
Greg Deardorff
Marty DeBow
Rick DeGroot
Bill Demersseman
Jeff DiMatties
Anthony Donaldson
Jeff Drake
Jay Dudley
Jeff Dunn
Maurice "Mo" Dunn
Rick Durrance
Ken Edwards
Dirk Elliott
David Ellis
Eddie Ellis
Glen Ellwood
Hon Eng
Mark Engler
Bill Evans
Mark Filonczuk
Brian Fink
Chris Fisher
Jeff Ford
Ben Foulk
David Fowler
Derin Fowler
John Fowler
Larry Fowler
Tom Fraley
Sam Fritz
Mac Fulcher
Doug Gamble
Vince Gappa
Ken Gavel
Roy Gearhart
Greg Gibson
Terry Gibson
Randy Gillett
Rick Givens
Grant Graff
Larry Green

Terry Greenlee
Hugh Griffith
Greg Groves
Mark Hale
Jack Hankins
Greg Hanks
Dirk Hansen
Casey Harding
Tom Harding
Matt Harmon
Mark Harris
Neal Hartzell
Tom Hauschild
Chuck Hawkins
Gary Hawkins
Bruce Hayes
Wylie "Buff" Hearn
Jeff Heath
Kent Hedlund
Denny Heiberg
Joe Henderson
Glenn Hendrix
Wayne Henegar
Wayne Hepler
Steve Heyduck
Chris Hill
Dan Hines
Mike Hinton
David Hodge
Audie Hodges
Phil Hogg
Mike Hoke
Mark Hollis
Jon Honda
Robert Hopper
Jeff Horton
John Hubbs
Bill Hughes
Dick Huston
Wes Irwin
Wyll Irwin
Jonathan Isaacs
Dan Jansen
Ken Johnson
Lon Johnson
Vic Johnson
Rob Jones
Gary Jones
Tom Kalina
Jim Kane
Bob Kaylor
Mike Kelly
Mark Kennedy
Wayne Kenney
Evan Kenyon
Bob Kidd
Bill Kierce
Chris Kiesling

Tom Kilburn
David King
Mike Knox
Dan Koehn
Jim Kraus
Charlie Kreuger
David Kubal
Mendall Kugler
Jim Leggett
Pete Legner
Mike Lehman
John Lemasters
Scott Leu
Phil Lewis
Robert Lewis
Greg Ligon
Steve Linder
Dale Locke
Steve Logsdon
John Long
Bill Love
Ken Love
Mark MacAdow
Bill MacDonald
Gerry McCall
David McCarthy
Billy McCauley
David McConnell
Christopher McConville
Doug McCormick
Tom McElroy
G.J. McGarvey
Mel McGinnis
Wes McIntryre
Rodney McKean
Bart McKelvey
George McKinney
Tim McKinney
Stan McKinnon
Bruce McLaughlin
Walter Marlowe
Jim Marshall
Gary Mason
Jerry Massie
Marty Mathis
Dan Maurer
Mike "Buzz" Maxey
Larry Mealy
David Meddars
Ralph Merante
Dale Mero
Tom Michalko
Gil Miller
Randy Miller
David Moehring
Richard Monroe
Jonathan Moore
Lynn Moore
Scott Morgan
Ron Morgan

Rich Morris
Carl Morton
Matt Mote
Michael Mudge
Gary Mulholland
David Murdoch
Bob Murr
David Murray
David Neckers
Rob Nicholson
Liam O'Byrne
Terry Otto
Jonathan Palmer
David Panther
Dan Parry
Randy Pasqua
Johnny Patterson
Steve Pavey
Steve Pescosolido
Rich Phipps
Steve Poekert
Carrol "Luch" Pope
David Powless
Rob Price
Sam Price
Barry Queen
Benjamin "Bo" Quigg
Bill Ranta
John Rech
Alan Retzman
Frank Reynolds
Don Richards
Shan Ricketts
Stephen Riley
Ed Ross
Eldon Sanders
Mike Sawyer
Darren Schaupp
Mike Schneider
Chris Schumske
Greg Scott
Steve Seamands
Bill Seitz
Smith Sharpe
Michael Shea
Rick Sheppard
Jack Shields
Brian Shimer
Lynn Shmidt
Joey Shuffett
Craig Sider
Mario da Silva
Don Sizemore
Duane Skene
Dan Slagle
T.J. Slocum
Brian Small
Brad Smith
Brent Smith
Dan Smith

Daryl Smith
Dean Smith
Eric Smith
Steve Smith
Tim Smith
Steve Somers
Don Spachman
Gordon Sparks
Albie Stadtmiller
Tim Stambaugh
Richard Stapleton
Bill Stegmueller
Tom Strickfaden
Randy Stringer
Jack Strong
David Swarbrick
Mike Tabb
Dean Taylor
Brook Thelander
Kevin Thompson
Rex Thompson
Mark Tidman
Ivan "Ike" Timm
Mark Tilley
Doug Timberlake
Adrian Timmons
Kevin Turner
Jim Tysick
Christian Ulrich
Kent Usry
Chip VanLandingham
Doug Vogel
Andy VomSteeg
Mel Vostry
Bill Wade
Mark Wade
Steve Waldorf
Greg Waldrip
Doug Walker
John Walt
Keith Wasserman
Ron Waughter
Dan Wayman
Dennis Wayman
Steve Wenzel
Carl Westbrook
Karl Westfall
Ken Werlein
Robert Whinnen
Ryan Wickman
Gene Williams
John C. Wilson
Keith Winslow
Karl Wolfe
Greg Wood
Greg Woods
Larry Wright
Ralph Yoder
Dean Ziegler

FOREWORD

I spent the first thirty-five years of my life, like most men in our competitive American culture, thinking success, fulfillment, and happiness would result from what I could achieve. My feelings of self-worth and my identity as a person were dependent on what I could *do* — first as a professional athlete, then on the sideline as a coach.

I've spent the last thirty-five years learning that God is far less concerned about what we *do* than He is about what we *are.* So what truly matters most in life is not our professional achievements, but our personal relationships — first with God, second in our families, and then with others we work and live among.

In all my years coaching football with the Dallas Cowboys, I've seen two common barriers that most often prevent people from experiencing the best in these relationships and often keep them from reaching their fullest potential in their professional lives as well. The first barrier is a pattern of past failure and past mistakes. The second thing holding people back is a fear of failure.

Don Joy tackles both these factors in *Men Under Construction.* He proposes concrete strategies for recognizing, understanding, and overcoming the crippling impact past mistakes can have on our lives and our relationships. Plus he lays a confident foundation of hope and faith for building whole, healed, successful, God-blessed lives and relationships.

I invested twenty-nine years of my life with the Dallas Cowboys, coaching, motivating, teaching, and leading men who came from a broad range of backgrounds and represented the full spectrum of personality types. Some exhibited a depth of character that quickly earned my admiration and respect. Others had problems and weaknesses that made them difficult to work with. But all of them—strong or weak, confident or insecure, good or bad—could have benefited from the principles Don Joy lays out in the following pages. Because all of us are men under construction. We all need a better understanding both of who we are and who God wants us to be.

I've known a lot of guys who have tried to prove themselves "a man's man." But it's so much more important to be "God's man." This book offers a well-thought-out game plan that will help you do just that.

Tom Landry,
Dallas, Texas

INTRODUCTION:
Coming Home to Integrity and Freedom

Five of us piled into my Caprice for the three-hour drive to Columbus, Indiana. I was making a "hit and run" banquet speech on family issues for a large congregation there, following it with a 90-minute seminar. I threw the invitation out to my early morning men's group, hoping for one guy to help me drive and keep me awake on the return trip. What I got were four who jumped at the opportunity.

For three hours the lively banter took us to the pinnacles of humor and laughter. It was as if we all knew we needed a "high" and this was the spontaneous "male medication" — jokes, pranks pulled long ago, everything calculated to boost us to yet another peak endorphin explosion cascading through our bloodstreams, elevating our immune systems and bolstering our good health.

We stepped out in front of impressive First Christian Church, scrambling to locate the right entrance to descend to the banquet which was just beginning. I had warned my hostess that my class schedule predicted a tight arrival squeeze.

Before the car doors had slammed, I suggested: "Think about how much fun we've had. Men everywhere in the world do the same thing—provoke each other to laughter by using old experiences and jokes to generate positive chemistry. It is a 'right brain deficit' that drives it, and stories trigger the images and emotions that make us thrive. But men whose only male contact is around jokes and laughter are always masking the real cry of their souls. Think about it. We've had two good semesters together and talked candidly about several issues, but left to ourselves, we go for the gusto of a good laugh."

I was not prepared for the mellow ride home. We hit the road. I had driven to Columbus, but I handed the keys to Jim as we crawled back aboard. Dave, Dan, and I piled into the backseat, and Liam rode shotgun with Jim. We all came out of that trust chamber with agendas to begin new and deep personal work. We have been doing it now for four years with the good support of each other. If the trip north felt like recreational male banter, the trip home turned out to be lifelong male bonding through candor, confidentiality, identification, and resolve.

When I think of full-spectrum males, the Columbus trip encapsulates the two opposing poles: the rib-poking, fun-loving man and the listening, honest man. Either pole, by itself, would leave a man impoverished. But happy is the man who, in a day's time, can play the strings of his harp with the full sweep of high sensation and the deep throb of shared confidentiality.

Integrity and freedom surely belong to men who play all of the strings of their manhood. They can draw the bow or hit the court in a high energy recreational blast as Jonathan and David must often have done as young friends. But they can also bite the dust and soak up each other's grief as David and Jonathan did when it was clear that their carefree days of friendship had come to an end. And they will find themselves taking joy in the knowledge that their own sons and daughters may soon join the panoply as families continue the tradition of trust and encouragement that good men forged in full-spectrum friendships. (By the way, you can review David and Jonathan's full-spectrum banter, intimate grief, and lifelong bonding in 1 Samuel 20.)

So here is *Men Under Construction!* The dedication, if you bothered to look at it, lists nearly 350 men who have spent

from one to six semesters in weekly support networks, mostly over brown-bag lunches or a simple breakfast snack. In
this book I've referred to such covenant groups with intentional shared-life agendas as "Contractor's Crews." Both
"construction" and "contractor" suggest positive, life-build-
ing images. For more than twenty years, I have spontaneously created environments into which men could walk and find
a light agenda that would tilt conversation and prayer toward
playing the strings of personal integrity and candor. And from
their first session, most of the men have been charged with
an increasing sense of their own worth and their own "constructive power" to be the man of their vision and of God's
calling.

When Robert Bly's "A Gathering of Men" aired with Bill
Moyers on PBS, I videotaped the program, and for two weeks
our men's group watched that conversation. Then, for another six weeks we reflected on what was awakened in us by the
Bly-Moyers exchange. I stopped by the bookstore and bought
a copy of Bly's *Iron John* on my next run to the airport for a
weekend away. On returning, I bubbled up some of the "Iron
John" fairy tale about the "boy with the golden hair" and his
amazing mentor. Jim Marshall was eager to read the book, so
I let it go with the stipulation that he sit down with me to "do
the theology of *Iron John*" when he finished.

Jim graduated that spring and by midsummer was im-
mersed in youth ministry 200 miles away. Then he phoned
from Oklahoma where his high-school students were working
alongside Native American teens in a week of mission. Jim's
voice had a tinge of mild panic as my phone message device
caught him: "They've asked me to handle one hour of teaching every day, and I didn't bring anything to run with. If you
can call me back in twenty minutes, I'll stick by this pay
phone. I need ideas." He left the number, but it was six
hours later when I got the message. I phoned Pam, back at
his home base and told her of the call and furnished numbers
where Jim could reach me for the next several hours. But Jim
didn't call.

Ten days later, I phoned late at night to find Jim at home.

He laughed. "The phone call was all it took," he said. "I suddenly realized that I had everything I needed, and it turned out to be a great week." I was seized with laughter, for Jim's story was so in keeping with Iron John's adventure: The Boy with the Golden Hair came to the edge of the forest and called for Iron John. When there was no immediate reply and no instant stallion beneath him as before, the Boy with the Golden Hair turned back toward duty only to find that his own "gimpy legged horse" was transformed into the best horse in the field. That was a wonderful revelation!

As I continue to travel, it is easy to connect now with these hundreds of graduates and to catch them in their careers and families. We can pick up six for brunch or a family out for dinner—in San Diego, Los Angeles, Dayton, or Rochester. We are not, as we say, "in touch" with each other on any consistent basis. But we are all free and getting on with life agendas, knowing that our long months of integrity and absolute trust and encouragement have given us energy and freedom to keep both our families and careers in clear priority.

We also know that we have this lifetime and the next to reconnect and carry forward what began in these intentional conversations where all of the issues of *Men Under Construction* surfaced and were gently hammered out. This book is, in a real sense, the gift of 350 men who continue to be in the real Contractor's Crew.

Donald M. Joy
600 North Lexington Avenue
Wilmore, Kentucky 40390
Phone 606/858-3817

CHAPTER ONE

DESIGN: MALENESS AND MANHOOD

I was thirteen years old when Mother and Dad brought David home — my new baby brother. David was actually born in the car alongside U.S. 283 south of Dodge City, Kansas. My dad never forgave Doc Adams for billing them for a full "delivery fee," after what he went through in the middle of a September night.

One day while changing David's diaper, I was startled to discover that my baby brother had a fresh scar runing from the base of his penis full circle vertically around his scrotum! *He's been cut!* I thought. The scar was so straight, it looked like it had been made with a knife. Red, bright, and fresh, it stood up in a ridge of freshly healed flesh, and extended up the bottom side of his tiny penis.

I was angry, flushed with resentment toward Doc Adams, who must have cut him. (Growing up on a farm, I knew about such cuttings of male animals.) But as I looked more carefully, I reasoned: there are no stitches, so Doc Adams didn't do it.

The scar was a mystery. I closed the fresh diaper and said nothing to anyone. But the bright red scar bothered me. I saw it often, and soon after when it occured to me to examine myself, I discovered that I carried an almost invisible matching mark. Not until I was past the age of fifty would I find an explanation for my little brother's scar so fresh and red.

THE MALE PHENOMENON

Eventually I changed a few other diapers, including those of our two sons, and later, our three grandsons. The same bright red scar was always there. But we didn't know how to talk about sexual anatomy. When physicians talked, they spoke in Latin anyway. Who of us was competent to carry on a conversation with a highly trained professional? Anyway, the typical doctor's response was always a condescending, "It's nothing to worry about." So the scar remained a mystery to me.

I had never then given a second thought to the fact that baby boys have breasts. Nobody can tell a baby boy from a baby girl with their diapers on, because the upper bodies look identical. Not until pubescence strikes will the musculature and body hair patterns mark visible physical differences.

The truth is that only the chromosomes are different—from conception. Any girl might have turned out to be a boy, and any boy might have gone on to be a girl, if it hadn't been for the father's chromosome contribution. The mother always "votes" for a baby girl by bringing an X chromosome in the ovum. So the father's sperm carries the sex-determining chromosome—a father's X agrees on a girl; Y demands a boy—and buries itself in the mother's egg. Still the baby's basic fetal structure is female: breasts, ovaries, vagina—the works! This is true even of X+Y chromosome boys-to-be.

It is striking to discover that the father's Y shows up in 165 conceptions demanding a boy compared to 100 conceptions in which the father's X chromosome agrees on creating a girl. When the Y chromosome gives the orders: "Customize this baby. Make it a male," it is always a "modification" command, since the basic model of the baby during the first trimester is that of a girl.

"Changing a baby" from the basic girl anatomy to boy anatomy is miraculous work. The most crucial period is between the ninth and twelfth weeks—when the genital structure is changed from girl to boy and the testicles drop outside of the body into the scrotum. Most miscarriages occur during this important developmental process, and of the 165 boys conceived compared to 100 girl conceptions, 60 of them will be lost to miscarriages, most in the crucial days at the end of the first trimester.

WHEN ADAM SPLITS

It has been a painful discovery for me, well past midlife, to discover that I misunderstood the doctrine of Creation. I had thought, all of my life, that God created a bachelor male and called him Adam. Now, forced by the sheer startling truth of human conception and sexual development to reexamine the Genesis account, I discovered that the same biological fetal development story is told there:

1. God created a solitary human, named Adam.

2. The solitary, though complete, state was "not good," because the Adam was alone.

3. God created community by forming woman and man from the same Adam.

So Creation revists every conception, and the chromosomes determine which half of the gender split to follow. Human sexual differentiation was not given to us by God because male-female sex was necessary for human reproduction. The original Adam was complete. But the account of sexual differentiation is told using the picture of God's scalpel making a surgical separation of female and male parts of Adam. The reason? God saw that "It is not good for the Adam [my translation] to be alone" (Gen. 2:18). Just as the Trinity dwells in holy community, so also the human "image-bearers" must yearn for and spend their lifetimes rehearsing "community." Sexuality is a major gift which awakens and drives that profound hunger in all of us.

When I first coined the term "splitting the Adam" to describe what God did surgically in Genesis 2, I thought I was capitalizing on nuclear language to generate a bit of humor. Imagine my surprise to learn that the word *atom* was brought into English from the same Genesis passage. The word often translated "dust of the earth" is *adamah,* and in the doctrine of Creation it speaks always of the close linkage of our humanity with the raw material of the planet. So both atom and Adam come from the Creation language: one for the human formed of the dust, and the other referring to the minutest particles of Creation material![1]

The ovary-looking pair of sexual organs in the undifferentiated baby will become ovaries in the female and testicles in the male. The testicles, which might have continued to develop as ovaries, will be transformed into a pair of sperm-producing factories which will turn out up to 300 million sperm per day for three or more decades of adult life. Immediately upon their alteration, the testicles begin to produce distinctly male hormones, including the powerful testosterone. This testosterone production is credited with the fact that mothers carrying a baby boy tend to experience more vigorous fetal movement than those carrying a baby girl.

The vaginal lips seal slowly to form the amazing "straight as a knife" red scar. The vaginal lips therefore form the sac or scrotum which houses the testicles. Only breast nipple skin has the same elastic capacity found in the vaginal lips and scrotum. The lips expand to "crown" the birthing baby, and the scrotum expands to cool the testicles in summer and contracts to warm them in winter—maintaining the essential temperature required for healthy, motile sperm.[2]

SINGLE-MINDED MALES

If the "common body" from which female and male emerge following conception and the first trimester of development strikes you as amazing, consider what happens to the human brain. The natural state of the human brain is female, again following the pattern we saw in genital development.

The male brain is modified—again in response to the father's Y chromosome which has joined the mother's X. This combination calls for the chemicals to alter the genital system, and at the sixteenth week of the pregnancy, the mother's androgens—now joined by the male hormones pumping from the tiny fetal testicles—go into customizing action again. This time they will masculinize the young boy's brain.

In God's design, all brains—female and male—carry millions of cells which are programmed to disappear when an "androgen bath" surges through the cranium.

In a very selective way, brain cells in the left hemisphere of the male brain are greatly reduced in number. An estimated 25 million neurological fibers which make up the corpus colossum disappear. This "specialization" of the male brain allows males to block out emotional paralysis in the face of danger, noise, and other distractions if something urgent needs to be done.

One of the most obvious "sex differences" families notice is that their sons who are right-handed tend to acquire speech more slowly and in smaller units, and are nine times more likely to have speech defects than their daughters. Left-handed boys whose speech production is sometimes in the right hemisphere tend to take off as quickly as their sisters in speech development and to write smoothly, compared to their right-handed brothers' often tortured and illegible penmanship.

While the specialization of the boy's speech and writing center is easily the most obvious effect of this amazing sexual modification, it is no more important than several other brain specializations. Look at them:

Visual processing. Males tend to have superior ability to develop eye-hand coordination. They invent games of competition and historically have excelled and competed using this uncanny "developable" ability which undergirds all kinds of marksmanship. Today's male fascination with computer games and video arcade prowess may be the most conspicuous display of this gift. This skill development stems from a three-dimensional-perception ability that seems typically to develop more powerfully in males than in females.

Not only may this visual differentiation gift show up in eye-hand coordination, but also in the superior ability to identify distance between oneself and an object suspended in air (e.g., a clothesline). It is this endowment that thrusts males almost magically into three-dimensional reasoning. While general arithmetic and math are basically two-dimensional, geometry, calculus, and other engineering-like higher maths require inferential reasoning based on the ability to "see" what is not visible. Standard IQ and SAT tests, which provide pictures of stacked oranges from which to infer the regular pattern and determine the number in the whole pile, measure this ability to do three-dimensional reasoning.

We may add to these male patterns of processing the additional feature of the female's reverse optic system in comparison to the male. She, for example, tends to suffer from night blindness while facing oncoming headlights and for a few seconds after they have passed. But he tends to reach for sunglasses in fighting daylight blindness. Here, as in so many ways, woman and man are mirrors of each other. Little wonder that as we contemplate the original Adam, it is true again that it still takes two to put a complete "one" together.

Reasoning. You can imagine that optical development affects how we gather information for thought. But once the information is in the brain, males tend to work it over in a single-minded way, using their logical and analytical processes. By largely shutting down their "feeling" hemisphere, men are able to concentrate in noisy environments, for example. When they are focused in this way, whether by choice or necessity, it may be very hard to "break through" their single-mindedness. Women, with the wonderfully fully connected corpus colossum, are more open to interruptions and more "whole-minded" in their responses. Taken as a group, women integrate feelings with logic, beliefs with reality, and worship with theological reflection more easily than men do. Music, prayer, and poetry put a man in his "right mind," so he is easier to "dialogue with," suggesting ways of encouraging men to switch off the intense "single-hemisphere" mode.

Emotions. Men are more at the mercy of their feelings, since right-handed, right-eye dominant men tend to speak from their logical analytical left hemispheres. They have to work harder to articulate their "right mind" where feelings, emotions, and experiences with God are processed. Since men are often slower to articulate love, affection, or belief in supernatural, nonlogical dimensions of spiritual reality, they tend also to be less able to guard against assaults on and manipulation of their emotions. While men are characterized as being unemotional, at times of great loss it is not uncommon for them to lose control and be unable to explain what triggered the feelings. Sometimes it is this fear of "losing control" that keeps men away from experiences which might nurture their gentler gifts.

Creativity. Men are capable of high emotion and profound belief in the numinous — the transcendent spiritual realities — but they are often unable to communicate verbally in describing the experiences that mean so much to them. They frequently resort to musical composition or performance, or to painting, drawing, or writing in order to express this bottled-up numinous or affective experience. One way to explain the preponderance of great male composers and artists would be to suggest that their enormous energies have built up to explosion force, which delivered masterpieces instead of day-by-day words of affection, anger, or worship and adoration.

Sexual attraction. When comparing males and females, perhaps less is known about the source of sexual orientation than any other of the brain's differences. Recent studies are throwing new light on the likely biological center of "sexual preference." And since the "standard model" brain is female, it may be very crucial that masculinizing the brain in the sixteenth to twenty-sixth week of fetal development be supported by every emotional, family, and medical support we can provide. The structure of the hypothalmus is being studied as the principal center of sexual orientation and arousal. Roger Gorski of the University of California at Los Angeles, for example, reports from cadaver brain studies that the anterior commisure — part of the corpus collossum — is 34 percent larger in homosexual-preference men than in heterosexual-preference men. If so, then the "androgen bath" that changes the female structured brain to a downsized, specialized male brain with several millions of cells destroyed may explain a fetal development accident.

An MIT-based conference on sexual differentiation in the brain reported a German study of World War II baby boys born in heavily bombed target cities. That study found that the critical sexual orientation weeks are the sixteenth to twenty-sixth weeks and that the incidence of homosexual preference was greater for men whose fetal development was in that crucial phase during heavy bombing raids. The report from MIT listed two medical obligations: (1) Diagnosis and prevention of androgen deprivation during this critical ten-week period in mothers pregnant with males. (2) Remediation for males so affected by prenatal androgen deprivation.[3]

We have know for nearly forty years that male sexual orientation is more complex and falls into a less clear set of options than the female's. Evidently, the degree to which a baby's brain is masculinized varies from child to child. If so, then the strength or weakness of any group of males' sexual preference might be expected to extend across a spectrum, even if all were predominantly committed to heterosexual practice. When you add the possibility that an occasional baby boy might slip through during a period of serious hormonal depletion, either from mother-stress or from her overproduction of estrogens, you might expect to find a baby with male genitals but with a brain that remains essentially female. In chapter 4, I will explore ways of nurturing masculinity in boys, since growing up male seems to be a bit more hazardous than is growing up female.

Since it is the brain that responds to the million stimuli that affect sexual response, we will not debate long about where sexual arousal begins. Jesus knew the brain was the most powerful sex organ when He cautioned about "looking in order to lust" for sexual kicks (Matt. 5:28). According to Jesus, mental or visual pursuit and desire to use a person's body for sexual pleasure amounts to emotional adultery. Jesus seems to have confronted the proud accusers of the woman caught in adultery in John 8 with some sort of accusation about "heart" adultery. "Let the one without sin cast the first stone!" He ordered.

Today we know that sexual arousal is set off when the brain releases a chemical which instantly blocks the flow of blood away from the genitals and nipples. The tissues then become engorged with blood. They remain rigid and blood-inflated until the imagination passes or is interrupted.

Speech. It is common that nine out of ten children in the speech pathologist's special group are boys. While emotional trauma may leave effects in speech, and physiological malformation may account for others, the larger portion of cases are boys suffering from damaged speech development because of the prenatal androgen brain bath. Occasionally, the speech irregularity or slow developing vocabulary are obviously housed in a little boy with a deeper than normal voice. In such cases the low voice is likely related to the strength of the androgen bath during fetal development. Boys, as a group, develop language more slowly than girls, have more speech and pronunciation problems, and are more vulnerable to stuttering, stammering, and other speech-interruption patterns.

TIGER IN HIS TANK

As a baby boy arrives in the world, his testosterone and other androgens are likely to promote a continued higher activity level when compared to girls of the same age. Indeed, *hyperactive* may be a word applied far too widely, since boys normally need more space and options for physical activity than do girls. Crowded classes at church or school are frequently the real culprit behind what Diane McGinness at Stanford University has noted as a conspiracy between mothers, teachers, and physicians to overprescribe medication for otherwise normal-activity-level boys.[4]

The young boy's hormonally fueled energy will link up by the onset of pubescence with his more explicit sexual energy. Unlike his sister, whose sexual development may be taken in stride as a rite of passage into adult fertility status, the boy is confronted with a very different task. He has management responsibility for external genitals which begin to present themselves with an astonishing capacity for pleasure and more than a monthly demand for release.

Those boys are blessed who understand their sexual development as God's majestic witness: the image of God invested in human sexuality. To the extent that any man celebrates fertility and sexual ecstasy as that sacred investiture, he is on a path of integrity and of exclusive covenant love—in the right time and with the other magnetic partner who carries the missing "image of God" for which he was born to yearn.

The sea of adolescent sexuality is difficult enough to navigate alone, especially for boys with no one to interpret God's image gift to them. So when young men or women are placed in a sexually seductive culture, they may become easy pawns for greedy adults who target them with product advertising, music, films, and television programming calculated to exploit their sexuality for corporate or private adult profits. And when human sexuality misses the "image of God" ecstasy and meaning, it tends to become "idolatry." Sex then becomes "god," and sexual activity tends to take on "a life of its own." Compulsive, addictive, promiscuous activities replace God's gift of "endorphin" highs, and the thrill of breaking rules and boundaries triggers "adrenaline" highs in the form of escapades where everybody loses, but the high is mistakenly considered "worth it" because it is so much "fun."

In my book, *Parents, Kids, and Sexual Integrity,* I offer families strategies for holding the cultural seduction at bay through the cultivation of significant family affirmations and decisions. But the bottom line is simple: Young males' biological makeup causes them to be extremely vulnerable to sexual seduction. On one hand, their sexual energy is packaged so that daily fertility production is wrapped in enormous potential for pleasure, and on the other, they are intuitively aware that they are made for one exclusive, lifelong relationship. Besides, the external and pleasure-sensitive male sex system teaches them the special problem of ecstasy associated with their male identity. Too often, the time between first ejaculation and probable marriage seems to span at least half an eternity. It is into this "adolescent crucible" that young men move. During this period there will be enormous challenges to their "image of God" vision—tests of will and integrity. And most young men will feel that they have failed, either through masturbation, sexual contact with other males, or through premature genital contact with females.

As we look at men under construction and appeal for family caution and care as they take on their "image of God, male" potential, their sexuality constitutes their major moral curriculum. If they are to become honest and vulnerable men, capable of intimacy and gentleness as husbands and fathers, they will have to pass the sexual integrity test.

To become productive men in their careers, with vision and single-mindedness in pursuit of goals, they will have to find ways of harnessing their supersonic "tiger in the tank." The lifestyle choices for male sexual integrity are simple: a covenant-exclusive marriage *or* absolute, sanctified-to-God celibacy.

Whatever the choice or circumstance, men under construction will always be responsible for investing the exploding sexual energy of their manhood with integrity. For those who find themselves without a vibrant marital partner with whom to build exclusive intimacy, integrity calls them to excellence by joining the ranks of the honest and abstinent heroes. Their sexual energy will drive ambition, productivity, creativity, and develop new frontiers of intelligence, service, and space. And whether intimately married or reflectively celibate, their "image of God" sexual identity will bless the whole community by its uncommon peace and grace.

HOW TO USE THE CHAPTER TIPS AND NOTES
At the end of each chapter you will find two sets of agendas. The first, "Do-It-Yourself Tips," will give you some private working instructions to get you "doing what you read." The second, "Contractor's Crew Notes," will be an agenda you can use with a cluster of men you want to come to trust as your support network. Remember that every man has a story to tell if you empower him to tell it. Regular support network conversations tend to transform any man. These agendas will match the chapters and may launch you into a lifelong security network of honest men who will know you and bless you profoundly for the rest of your life.

Do-It-Yourself Tips

If you, like most of us, grew up feeling shame about your male sexual identity, try this "mirror talk." It is based on the fact that God has mysteriously created you so that your sexuality is God's "image" stamped into you. This will mean that if you listen, God's "Word has become flesh" in your sexuality, in your sensations, and in the empowering for creative reproduction. Most sexual disorders are directly motored by shame and a feeling that sexuality is somehow evil, solid trouble, or a source of negative "tension."

Lock the door then, facing yourself as a sexual person. You may stand, flex, kneel, sit, or all of the above while asking these questions: "What does it mean, God, that my sexuality is Your image in me—TO ME? TO OTHER PEOPLE? How can I handle this supersonic energy You have pumped into me? What does this hunger for pleasure and ecstasy tell me about You? How can I package myself as male and masculine in ways that match Your model of honesty, fidelity, and consistent goodness? Can you 'sanctify' my sexuality so my 'image' of You glows, shines, and tells the world what fidelity means?"

Contractor's Crew Notes

Pull your group of network men together after they have read this chapter, or after you have summarized the chapter for them. I call this section "Contractor's Crew Notes" because good men's networks must be under "contract" for regular and vulnerable participation, and you are a "crew" in the sense that you are on the most important "construction job" on earth: becoming honest and godly men. So contract with them for regular time together and for vulnerability.

You cannot simply ask for confidentiality, but you can guide your crew into progressive depths of sharing. As the agendas get more and more revealing, you will want to caution, in the words of Jesus, "Do not cast your pearls before swine." This means that anybody's pain must be carefully received, or the person will feel violated, mutilated, and the precious secrets will have been wasted and trampled on the floor.

The convenor or a rotating "facilitator" needs to lead off, completing the task before offering the time and space to each person present, one by one. It is OK to "pass," but most men will welcome a chance to revisit their own history. Share these early life episodes, once around the circle for each item:

1. "My first and best memory of 'being a boy and being proud of it' was when. . . ." [Be specific, tell your age, the event, who was there, what was said, and what you felt. Make your story live and coach everybody with questions to get the specific story images out for everyone to enjoy.]

2. Describe how your maleness or sexuality was a factor in sending you in search of God. [Was it a trigger for hungering for God and meaning? Was it guilt for fear you had mismanaged your sexual gift? Was it the awakening of a cosmic loneliness and a yearning for intimacy Somewhere with Someone?]

Read Psalm 139 or at least verses 1-4; 13-16; and 23-24. Do a football huddle or other appropriate masculine prayer posture and seal your stories between each other and before God.

CHAPTER TWO

DEFORMITY: FATHER TO SON?

My wife Robbie and I were the guests of Dan and Jan Johnson one evening not far from Princeton Seminary where he was completing the doctorate and where I was a summer "guest professor." There are few pleasures better than catching a glimpse of "the next generation" when you are with people you admire. The highlight of our time together was watching their young son Derin at play.

Derin, then about five years old, gave us a demonstration of his pre-Little League skills. His athletic endowments, even at that young age, were already visible. But as Dan pitched a dozen balls so we could watch the eye-hand coordination of young Derin's batting, we noticed that before each ball was released, Derin tucked his head forward over his left shoulder and released a tiny fleck of spit. Only then could he flex into position to assess the coming ball.

Back inside the house, I asked Dan about Derin's spitting ritual.

"I'm afraid he came by that honestly. It's something I do, and he watches all of the church-league games. I'm sure he thinks it is the essential trademark of being a Johnson at the plate."

In a recent semester I announced to each of my four men's network groups, consisting of about ten men each, that we would spend the next three months drawing on stories about our relationships with our fathers. Reading the *Chicago Tribune* story of Ken Druck's "Alive and Male" seminars, I decided to open the father subject with my forty men. Druck had found that men with unfinished business with their fathers tended to be "frozen up" in their emotions and relationships with their wives.

On the opening day, I spun out a story focused on my relationship with my dad during junior high. The agenda set off shock waves inside a couple of the participants. They made immediate appointments and came to see me privately.

"This is scary," Dale said. "Before it's time for me to talk about my father, I need to try to tell you privately about some of the things I'll have to share." Will reported, "My wife has been telling me that my bad temper with her is rooted in my anger and resentment toward my father. Can we talk about it before I open this up with the group?"

Men with a damaged father connection tend to be healed only to the extent that they can describe the loss and the pain in some confidential social arena. A support network group— what I've called in this book a "Contractor's Crew" for men under reconstruction—is the best environment for this. It is often superior to getting private therapy, primarily because the healing accelerates with this wider human social support base. Another support group advantage is that every story tends to trigger parallel experiences in the other participants. Instead of feeling isolated, each truth-teller discovers that his individual pilgrimage is enriched and mirrored by this band of fellow pilgrims with whom he is "under contract."

Children with damaged or lost relationships with either parent have a strong internal agenda which drives them to try to establish a surrogate connection. Sometimes it is found in a neighbor. That was Dale's case: "My father was home, but he had no time for me and showed no affirmation or affection to me. I actually was raised by the guy across the street. He had a son my age, and I guess it wasn't too much trouble for him to do everything with two of us instead of his son alone. That neighbor today remains my model of manhood and fathering."

Father loss, whether by death, abandonment, desertion, or divorce evokes a deep grief. Yet sometimes grief is short-circuited or choked, and remains in the denial stage. Gerry found himself simultaneously enrolled in a course on death and dying, and in my "Discipleship Development in the Family" class, where we opened the windows on childhood disruptions that are common in families. Subjects included "father absence." Here he was, a fully developed adult, put in touch with a grief that was buried back at age seven. Within a few weeks, he was able to link that loss to a small cluster of baffling fears and negative compulsions. A support network of trusted peers can bear the burden of grief shared at any stage or season of life.

Dan, abused by an alcoholic father, then rejected by a stepfather, despaired of being able to be a decent father to his own children. He had wandered through his college and seminary years largely as a loner. I found this treasure of a young man in a summer camping course, where he displayed absolute magic in working with troubled teenage boys. No wonder! He was working out of the authority of his own painful childhood. As his story began to surface, I invited him into a support network group where his scarred past continues to be healed.

Unlike Dan, most children reach out to replace a missing or a dysfunctional father. The church, school, and community environments tend to offer candidates for this reverse adoption. If we better understood how to be surrogate parents, we might better recognize a child's reaching-out signal. Accordingly, we would staff our agencies and classrooms more intentionally with magnetic and available adults. Ideally, we would train volunteers and employees in day-care centers, schools, and church agencies — equipping them to identify and provide potential surrogate fathers for those growing numbers of children whose homes are father-absent.

Listen to David's description of what Robert Bly calls "too little Father" in too many adult men today: "For myself and many others I've talked with about their fathers, our fathers have been there for us physically but not emotionally. A word picture comes to mind: Often I have felt like a book Dad placed on display on the coffee table. From the outside, the book may look interesting but actually it's never been opened and read through to really know what it's all about. I have felt this way with my father. He knows what I'm about on the outside, but he really doesn't know who I really am. In turn, I really don't know who he really is on an emotional level. He's been absent from my emotional life even though he was there physically."

David, and many of us, may discover that "Dad did everything for me that was essential. He was there. He demanded responsibility from me. He disciplined me. He coached me in facing my problems at school and in the world. He never hugged me. OK. But he gave stability and order to my life."

Since fathers are responsible for the "underside" of our lives, we often turn to father surrogates or to mentors for the blessing we need as emerging men, boys budding into full ripening. A father surrogate must take responsibility for discipline, duty, and training. Such a man rarely can also serve as the external "praise center" all of us need. So when a man can accept the imperfect and limited role fathers do pretty well — the coaching, shaping-up, advising services — he can search for the ideal man in a mentor.

Mentors cannot be our "blessors" if they have to discipline us, reprimand us, and pay our bills. The magic of a mentor is directly in porportion to the positive friendship and admiration that gets expressed "both ways." When a mentor turns into a critic, like the father, he tends to be rejected and another "parenting" grief is underway.

FATHERS AS FATHER

Both our culture and our genes combine to give us a sense that our fathers make and control our destinies. David McKenna, president of Asbury Theological Seminary, unpacked the "father connection" in a theological dimension for me as he offered a biblical exposition of Mark 1:11. His address at the 1983 annual campus ministers' conference was entitled, "Jesus' Credentials for Ministry: Affirmed by God." In that address, he illuminated with his own story the words of God the Father delivered through an angel as Jesus came out of the water at His baptism, "This is My Son, whom I love; with Him I am well pleased" (Matt. 3:17).

McKenna asserted that God's affirmations were sweeping:

> I claim you. I love you. I am proud of you. Everyone needs to belong, to be loved, to be praised. When God says, "I claim You," Jesus finds the strength of His identity. When God says, "I love You," He finds the strength of His security. And when God says, "I'm proud of You!" He has His sense of worth. This is the unshakable identity that Jesus took as His credential into His public ministry. We, too, need these strengths of personhood. These are the relational credentials we must have if our ministry is to be effective: a sense of identity, of security, and a sense of self-worth.

To drive home the importance of these words from the Father to the Son, McKenna put hundreds of clergy into a breathless trance by noting the probability that in such a gathering there would be people stung by abandonment and by the wounds lingering after parental divorce or other father-absence issues.

Then he confided, "I personally know a bit of that hurt and I can speak about it, because I can feel those wounds." He unfolded the story of his father's announcement to him at a drive-in restaurant that he was leaving his mother for another woman. "Then digging deeper, he told me that he had married my mother only to give me a name. The bond between us was cut for the next fifteen years." McKenna reports that the bond was repaired finally in a reconciliation when he was able to say, "I love you!" just before his father died.

McKenna went on, "Perhaps that is why my proudest moments are when I introduce my children. I love to say 'This is my son!' or 'This is my daughter!' I want the whole world to know that I love them, that they are mine, and that I am proud of them. We belong to each other!"

The loss of a father, devastating as it is for both sons and daughters, seems to do the greatest damage to the boys. They typically are assigned, or abandoned by the father, to remain with the mother. Thomas Parish's finding about the dynamics of divorce demonstrate a pattern few of us would have guessed. If the mother's fortunes improve after the divorce, the boys's sense of self-worth diminishes. If she enjoys fewer comforts and life gets tougher, the boy's self-worth rises. Evidently sons are so attached to their fathers' identities and sex roles that they are watching a subtle "stock market" to see whether males have any real value.[1]

If any blockage settles down between a father and a son, whether by divorce or abandonment, the son very often sets out to prove his own worth—to somehow catch the attention and approval of his absent father. Some of the highest motivation ever studied is in these driven men.

Mack appealed to me during his college freshman year. He was still suffering from the messy expulsion he had survived when his father had put an ultimatum to him the day the divorce was final: "You decide whether you want to be with me or with your mother. If you choose her, I will never speak to you again. You will no longer be my son." Mack and his sister, Melody, chose to stay with their father. A younger brother went with their mother. The expulsion came during the summer after Mack had graduated from high school. One day his dad walked in and found Mack talking on the phone long distance to his mother. "I'll give you twenty-four hours to be out of here." So Mack packed suitcases, a few boxes, and a gigantic trunk and was off for his mother's place until college. I met him only a few weeks after he had entered college.

Five years later, with a mounting log of father rejection of his efforts to write, phone, and send Christmas gifts and seasonal greetings to his father, Mack unveiled the anguish to the brown-bag-lunch support group. Across the years, Mack had meticulously organized his life. And his aspirations were well above "mere survival." He worked for his own support, persistently pulled down top grades, ran for campus office, and carried on a "high-fidelity" weekend ministry. Mack also courted and married. Now with a baby just arrived, he was exploding. He told us why.

"Eileen's family is so supportive. And my mom and her husband are easy to deal with. But we decided that when the baby was born we would notify all three households, even though my dad has not spoken to me, written, or phoned since he put me out five years ago. When my sister reported unopened Christmas gifts I had sent six months after they were stale, I should have known not to try to call. But we made up three slips of paper with their names on them, to see who we would call first. Dad's name came up first. I have never even seen the woman he married after I left home. But I called.

"Dad answered the phone. I said, 'Congratulations! You are a grandfather for the first time!' He did not respond. I heard him breathing, then there was the click of his receiver and the dial tone in my ear. I thought I would die. But I turned to face the window so Eileen couldn't see my face, and I manufactured a fake one-sided conversation—a short one—to mask from Eileen this further rejection and rudeness of my father."

Emotional abandonment can occur with the victim remaining under the same roof. Sons' unfinished business with their fathers often centers around feelings that they are worthless—as proved by their father's rejection. When parents divorce, it is common that adult sons and daughters are devastated. The entire legal basis for their conception has collapsed, so they often feel they have entered into a new domain of emotional abortion or illegitimacy—surviving "out of wedlock" at best, "without a reason for being" at worst.

"My dad was my best friend until I was twelve years old," Bill told the whole class. "He taught me how to do everything around the place, plus fishing, overhauling motors— everything. But when I was about twelve years old he abandoned me—he pulled away. It was like I frightened him or something. So I was vulnerable to the whole scene of the city—the sex, drugs, and alcohol that were everywhere. He didn't help me deal with any of them and he knew I was a sitting duck for all that stuff."

Fathers with unfinished business of their own often shut down. Some are simply ignorant; no one ever took them into maturity as responsible men either. Others become entangled with compulsive alcohol, drugs, sex, or other addictions. A growing boy on the premises is often a reminder of the father's lost youth, vitality, good looks, and hope. That jealousy for lost vitality and youth can shut down the comradeship that was present during childhood. And for still other fathers, the son's emerging manhood can quicken the flesh of the father's lost youth, causing the father to move into the fast track of midlife misadventure—sexual infidelity, perhaps even promiscuity. The silence which follows is the visible mask for the father's guilt and shame. King David's affair with Bathsheba and his ordered murder of her husband came, significantly, as David's young sons were embracing their manhood. These events were the obvious triggers for wave after wave of their young adult escapades of incest, rape, and additional murder.

There is little doubt that unfinished business with fathers is men's number-one agenda. To be a boy is to aspire to grow up to be a father. The adoration flows inevitably from a son to his dad.

DISPOSABLE FATHER?

Yet fathers, with all of that clout and power in the family structure, are virtually powerless to maintain contact with a wife or a family if the mother chooses to abolish his role and relationship. Courts in the Western world consistently award children to the custody of mothers. Men may provide sperm for birth and money for sustenance, but they are easily cut out of the lives of their children. Listen to the worst possible case as George Gilder describes the role of the male in his *Men and Marriage:* "Although the man is needed in intercourse, artificial insemination has already been used in hundreds of thousands of cases. Otherwise, the man is altogether unnecessary. It is the woman who conceives, bears, and suckles the child."[2]

In this updated edition of his earlier *Sexual Suicides,* Gilder spins a theory by which he sees men, historically, as sexually inferior to women. Whereas a woman's sexuality drives her total life, men tend only to be marginally and occasionally sexual, their sexual appetite having little to do with most of their day-by-day work and survival. In this sense, Gilder suggests, mothering is a global and total task compared to fathering, which is more occasional and episodic. Men, Gilder says, are made "equal" by social conventions. He thinks it is not surprising that men have taken a firm grasp on the legal domain, at least partly to control and protect this fragile role that men have when they are reduced to fertilization services alone.

Gilder suggests it is men's strength, unequaled by the average woman, and men's ability to win food money in the marketplace with which males have made a deal with women. In exchange for her comfort, care, and intimacy, he can promise to honor, protect, and provide for her and their children.

Gilder's social-biological theory is chilling, but it underscores the vulnerability of males. They may be exiled out of intimacy, marriage, and family at the whim or legal maneuvering of a woman. Their dominance is plausibly rooted in this insecurity, so women suffer from malevolence and insensitivity as a male strategy to maintain control from their intrinsically weaker position. Relationships, especially marriages, which are plagued by these dynamics put both men and women in no-win situations.

FATHERS OMNIPOTENT
"My daddy is bigger than your daddy!" The childhood taunt focuses on the "super-person" in a little boy's world. Fathers earn their domain, at least in the little boy's eyes. Who can free stuck windows, open stubborn jars, or untangle impossibly confused fishing line? Daddy, of course. To whom does Mom and the whole family turn when the going gets tough? Wait, of course, until Daddy gets home, and he will fix it.

So, accustomed as men are to indulging in this microcosm of omnipotence, they tend to wade fearlessly in on any problem assuming that they, indeed, can fix it. There is a curious and almost exclusively male impulse to fix things. Men tend to assume whenever a problem or pain arises that they are expected to fix it. They are typically more interested in fixing things than asking questions, listening, sympathizing, or grieving with people who want simply to know that they are there and that they care about the people involved in an unfixable situation.

This male omnipotence tendency is grounded in the fact that male musculature accounts for 42 percent of his adult body, compared to about 20 percent musculature of an adult female's. Males are equipped to make a major contribution through their strength, prowess, and protection. But when such display of male strength is deformed, motivated by insecurity, or marshalled to mask feelings of inferiority, it can become abusive, cocky, or violent to destructive extremes.

FATHERS OMNISCIENT

The same insecurity that may drive a father or any male to dominate, to assume that they are responsible for fixing everything, also drives dogmatism—the closed mind. The husband of a woman who looks to him for all wisdom, either out of reverence and respect, or out of seductive "weakness" and her luxury of being a "kept woman," will easily fall into the trap of becoming the omniscient, all-wise decision maker.

Both pagan and naive religious traditions tend to exalt male omniscience: "Isn't the man supposed to be the head of the house?" is a common question among them. Both women and men ask the question. Yet the Scriptures nowhere speak of male "headship" to suggest that men omnisciently rule or have dominion over women. God's "dominion" command in Genesis is to "them"! "Let them have dominion . . ." is the original command, namely: "Take charge! Be responsible!" But it is a joint-tenancy and co-regency charge explicitly to both male and female in the image of God.

The Apostle Paul advises children, "Obey your parents in

the Lord, for this is right" (Eph. 6:1), but no passage of Scripture calls for *obedience* of wives to husbands or husbands to wives. Translators have to repeat the verb in Ephesians 5:22, "Wives *submit* to your husbands..." to make it demand unilateral submission of women to men. Verses 21 and 22 should actually read, "Submit yourselves to one another out of reverence for Christ. Wives, to your husband as to the Lord."

The italicized "submit" in 5:22 of the *New American Standard Version* does not mean "emphasize this." Instead, it is the translators' way of telling us that "submit" is actually not in the oldest and best texts, but had to be added to provide a verb for the new sentence they arbitrarily invented. And when you consider that the *New International Version* translators not only added a verb but broke the narrative and placed the "Wives and Husbands" subhead between that section and the overarching commands regarding "mutual submission" as God's design for the Spirit-controlled life, you suspect that the translators were being driven by a male-control political agenda.

Paul's use of "head" is consistently *cephale*, or a literal anatomic head which is useless and dead unless it is connected to a healthy body. The passage climaxes by citing Eden and the "two [head and body/man and woman] becoming one." So the Ephesians material holds up both Eden's "two became one" and also offers the new "head and body" image of a whole person who is healthy, in unity, and able to accomplish tasks with the full energy of head and body synchronized. The opposite—a "chain-of-command marriage"— would suggest a power control and even an adversary position. Marriage then would look spastic, and when Jesus is separated from the church, His body, by neurological damage, we have a spastic church.

Only the docrine of the Fall, as recorded in Genesis, names a top power position for the man. But "He will rule over you" (Gen. 3:16) is not God's order for marriage or the family. It is a curse and a consequence of the Fall, not God's norm for relationships. We should repent of and resist this negative pull of sin instead of baptizing the urge to dominate and calling it "the Christian marriage." The idea of "head" denotes a fragile but indispensable contribution which a man makes to the "total person," of which the wife is the "body." The total person requires absolute health and synchrony between head and body, between the man and the woman. What a pity it would be to have a spastic marriage, a head and body uncoordinated through consensus. The Creation gift of domination was to "them" (Gen. 1:28). The domination mandate over creation is in the immediate context of God creating them male and female in His image and turning the creative management of the rest of creation over to them.

Male omniscience is a heavy mantle to wear, and it assigns or accepts responsibilities no human can execute satisfactorily. Some men may come close to perfection, but the lone-ranger-executive male frequently carries the wounds of his wrongly accepted domain: hypertension and heart disease.

Since men are physically endowed to be primitive bread-winners and muscle-based providers, they once tended to dominate exclusively in a world where knowledge and wisdom were essential for survival. It is easy to see that the hunter-warrior-gatherer male might be looked to by women and children as the wizard of the wild world. But today, things are different: women as well as men work widely and have communication access to the entire global village.

Still, in many families, the myth of the omniscient male remains virtually unchallenged, however damaging it is to everyone in the family. And in parts of Western culture where hunting and gathering are no longer possible, women work to support unemployed and indigent males whose narrow definition of masculinity has disenfranchised them from the human species. They turn to violence on the streets, to compulsive addiction to illegal and destructive substances, and otherwise become caricatures of "the image of God, male."

A young man growing up today is exposed to powerful but contradictory messages about what is intrinsically masculine. The exaggerated omnipotence-omniscience model remains in many pagan and religious communities, and it always shows up in the survivalist and cultic camps which practice racism and elitism. Unfortunately, the more flexible biblical vision of man and woman in union forming the whole person is often lumped with a radical feminism which demands an end to male dominance and seeks to create a woman's world where men are reduced to indentured sperm-bank donors. This misunderstanding fails to take into account the distinct differences between the biblical pattern for relationships and the presuppositions of the radical feminists.

SONS OF THEIR FATHERS

Watch any young boy imitate Dad talking or walking, and you get a clue into the powerful imprint fathers make on their sons. To be a boy is to be in the image of Daddy, to want more than anything else to grow up to be like Dad.

Harry Chapin's popular song of some years back, *The Cat's in the Cradle,* is a haunting parable of son imitating father. In it Chapin sings of a father who had no time for his son as a little boy or teen, and eventually discovers as he grows older that his son can't find time for him either.

When a father habitually neglects, criticizes, or rejects a son, a powerful and destructive message is turned loose. Adult children of alcoholics, for example, are a group who have to deal with the lifelong effects of damage to the core of personality. It is most visible in devastated self-respect. If that respect was not filled up by a consistent, affirming, and fair father, it will take a network of friends in the adult years to fill the damaged cup of self-respect. The cup is not only empty, but it has developed a "hole" which prevents the affirmation of others from beginning to fill it. Daddy's negative evaluation outweighs them all.

In Arthur Miller's play, *Death of a Salesman,* Willy Loman is the idol of his wife, Linda, and the rising star of his two sons, Happy and Biff. They imagine that he is the most successful salesman in the world and that when he dies famous people will grieve his death.

This ideal father image is put in the fiercest artistic spotlight when Biff misses graduating from high school by four points on his math final exam. Willy is selling in Boston, so Biff hitchhikes there to find the hotel where his father always stays. Biff knows that Dad can get "Old Birnbaum" to change that grade. Finally, he finds the room but has a hard time getting Willy to answer the door. After carefully hiding a prostitute in the bathroom, Willy finally faces Biff at the door. But when Biff cracks a joke, she laughs and the secret is revealed. Biff's vision of Willy is immediately shattered. Willy takes over and violently demands that Biff and he go home to talk Mr. Birnbaum into giving Biff the points he needs to graduate.

Biff, seeing his father for who he really is, explodes, "He [Mr. Birnbaum] would never listen to you. . . . You fake, you phony little fake! You fake!"

Years later, a perplexed Willy asks longtime neighbor Bernie, who grew up with his son, whatever happened to Biff.

"It's like something hit him like a hammer, and he laid down and died! He never accomplished anything after he flunked math," Willy whines.

But Bernie's reponse angers Willy. He pointedly recalls the time that Biff literally gave up on life. He then asks Willy Loman the most penetrating question of the entire drama, "What happened up in Boston when Biff went looking for you?"[3]

Boys need their father's blessing and their fidelity to the naive ideal of childhood adoration. But any form of dishonesty between father and son sets an agenda of profound trauma that frequently haunts the adult life of the son, often damaging his aspirations, marriage, and parenting behavior.

Jeff's story is a mirror of such behavior: "I can't believe how messed up Dad is. I have two older sisters, and he has made life miserable for all three of us. Mom sees what he is doing to us. I called home over last weekend, for example, and he started up a big fight. So when I finally hung up at the end, I just felt terrible, like 'What's the use of living, if I'm as worthless as he says?' "

Jeff was a handsome young man, single, and in the prime of

young life—just under twenty-five. I had never seen him before, and my sign-up sheet was filled when he really needed to talk the week before. But here he was in my office now, with a question about his paralyzed life of prayer. I turned the question into explorations about his relationship with his father.

I asked Jeff how his father treated people outside of the family. He responded, "Wonderfully. In fact, he is very popular in our home community. He teaches physical education, and all the students love him. I have watched him deal with his gym class and with regular classroom students. He treats them like royalty—he's really gracious and affirming with them. But something happens when he gets home; he treats us all unbelievably shabbily."

"How does he treat your mom?"

"Like she was his mother or something—no magnetism that I've ever seen. He cares *about her,* but not *for her,* I think. And he's rude to her sometimes, but it's like he knows he better not bite the hand that feeds him."

"And how does he treat you and your sisters?"

"My sisters are married, so the relationship has changed. Dad is basically your decent, civil person. He shows off well in public, and dishes out money when we need it."

"Is he picking up the tab on your tuition and living expenses now?" I inquired.

"No. Mom works and she's helping me. I'm sure none of his money goes to pay any of my bills. When I'm home, though, he will pull out his wallet when I am leaving and hand me a twenty or a couple of them."

"Is your dad available at important times? Is he predictably there," I asked Jeff, "or does he have a habit of missing the important things in your life? Will he come to your graduation here, for example?"

"He'll be here, and everybody will think he's a wonderful guy. When he was at my ball games, for example, he was really cool. My friends thought I was really lucky to have a dad like that. It was when I got home that he lit into me, always criticizing and humiliating me in front of the family.

He always called me awful names—unbelievable and despicable ones. I was really confused by that, because he seemed to like me when I was with my friends. I'm thankful for that. He didn't embarrass me in front of my friends. But sometimes I think I must be losing my mind, to have had such terrible experiences with this man behind closed doors at home."

"Tell me about your mom," I continued with Jeff. "How does she deal with your dad?"

"She manages very well. And she tells us she is sorry that we don't see Dad at his best, that really he is a very good person. We are right, she says, to be angry at the way he is putting us down all the time, and she wishes we would stand up to him some way.

"I remember she has often told me in one way or another, 'Don't grow up to be like your daddy.' That has been the hardest thing to handle. There is so much about him that I admire, but at home he's a jerk. So I've been close to my mother. She says she has tried to tell him how he has mistreated us by ruthlessly criticizing and humiliating us."

Biff in *Death of a Salesman* and Jeff both carry symptoms of what Dan Kiley calls the "Peter Pan Syndrome" in his book of the same name. The most visible symptom is their social paralysis. These Peter Pans seem unable to enter into full adult male responsibility—a subtle point made in the *Peter Pan* musical where the play calls for a girl to play the Peter Pan role in an effort to show a "boy" with unchanged voice and childhood immaturity. These "Peter Pan" adult men suffer from shattered self-respect, insecurity, from watching an unpredictable father, and feelings of having been betrayed by him. All of this has damaged the sense of self.[4]

Whether we think of that damage as being to the "inner child of the past," or the "figurine within," or as a "hole in the soul," the painful imagery tells it all. The damage is early and deep, and is the root of symptoms he will bear in the adolescent and adult years. Most of these disappointing fathers were themselves damaged in their childhood. At some level the wounded sons and the damaged fathers are both victims. But we can trace this trauma with fathers, typically, across four or five generations before the dramatic effects begin to fade—unless one man says "enough is enough! I will end this stupid cycle."

Exodus 20:4-6 states the taboo against "idolatry," and follows with an explanation about the "Peter Pan" effect:

> You shall not make for yourself an idol in the form of anything in heaven above or on the earth beneath or in the waters below. For I, the Lord your God, am a jealous God, punishing the children for the sins of the fathers to the third and fourth generation of those who hate Me, but showing love to a thousand generations of those who love Me and keep My commandments.

Are we describing "idolatries" of confused priorities or hidden "gods" who control fathers? And do these priorities constitute "hating" God by ignoring the father tasks and the path of repentance that would bring wholeness in a single generation to stop the chain-effect devastation from father to son to grandson?

It is not surprising that Kenneth Druck reports from his "Alive and Male" seminars that men's pain about unresolved issues with their fathers is the most persistently recurring emotional block in their lives. Druck reports that the men in his seminars were eager to talk about their fathers. He discovered that while most men carry vestiges of an unresolved past, they needed someone else to prime them for a reconciliation. Thus, his seminar thrives with its primary focus on men's unfinished business with their fathers.

For example, if men are unable to express feelings to their wives, the roots seem to be in the father connection. If they can acknowledge and verbalize deep feelings about their fathers, their emotions revive and they reenter the human race as changed men.[5]

Evangelist Bill Glass, speaking to a businessmen's luncheon in Fort Wayne, Indiana, told of his visits behind prison bars. Glass has been admitted to more prisons than any other guest speaker. He asserted that he has not met one man in prison who has feelings of respect or affection for his father. Instead, hatred, resentment, and indifference express the full range of negative feelings he finds among convicted prisoners toward their fathers.

In my book, *Bonding: Relationships in the Image of God,* I report the key question I use when anyone expresses a fading belief in God: "Tell me about your relationship with your father." Indeed, it was that question which unraveled Jeff's story about his father. Jeff had made his urgent appointment with me to tell me he could no longer pray. I'm sure he thought I had not heard his confession when I followed it quietly with the question, "How are you getting along with your father?" Jeff's story emerges again in chapters 6 and 7.

Except for intentional seminars and the rare support groups a few men cultivate, many get in touch with their feelings through the mask of alcohol or street drugs. Men can talk about painful agendas over beer. They can even embrace each other in the bar. If they break through the boundaries of social propriety in talking or touching, they can always disclaim the event: "I was a little drunk." Unfortunately, the anesthesia strategy of using alcohol to mask the intimate truth-telling lets men down when they are sober again. Afterward, they are only humilated and ashamed in new ways. They find themselves having to return to a reality which demands that they deny the feelings they expressed when they were out of control.

I have found that men can tell the deep truth best in a support network which has an open agenda of truth-telling and confidentiality. Without that, many men wither and hide their deepest questions and fears. Others seek out the superficiality of macho adventures which have gestures of unbridled and uncensored speech. But those verbal salvos are rarely honest and are often laced with alcohol as a self-medication for deep inner anguish which remains unresolved. But in a lightly structured men's group dedicated to the proposition that all men are "under construction," they can plumb the deepest subjects. They can embrace and revive stifled feelings locked inside when mutual respect and full participation in a common agenda create the necessary confidential setting.

This chapter has opened the windows to look at the "father connection." Every man longs to be connected to an ideal father. That is tremendously good news. Boys keep an eye on the male high-school teacher, youth worker, or professional athlete. The secret behind this search is likely this: God has invested one version of His image in the human male. There is only one perfect Father, and all of us who are human fathers are only "images," flawed and imperfect, of the One who has no flaw and no peer. But because of the mystery of God's creation, every human male is "imaging" God to himself and to everybody else. So, take heart, your "image" is showing, and it has enormous potential for making God's "very good" statement to everyone who knows you.

Do-It-Yourself Tips

Check the mirror as you shave. With the door locked, look into your eyes and see whether you have your father's eyes. Check your hands. Are they carbon copies of his?

Have you talked to your father this week? Do you keep in touch with him? What "father energy" are you drawing on as an adult in your continuing relationship? Do you carry pain or trauma from father neglect, father abuse, father failure? Buy a card, write a letter, or make a phone call to Dad today.

If your father no longer is alive, or if you are permanently estranged from him, take longer on the eyes and review the "best moments" in memory. Then give yourself permission to grieve the loss of your father. Ask who the "surrogate dads" were for you and bless them while you reconstruct special and empowering moments in the relationships. Then, reflect on your special mentor, the man who blessed you and empowered you for career, for manhood, for marriage, and for fathering.

Make two or three phone calls: substitute dads, mentors,

and a peer who helped you to define yourself as a man. Spread around a little "male blessing"!

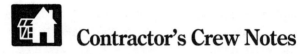 ## Contractor's Crew Notes

Open the "father story" at this session of your "under construction" Crew. Remember? The facilitator comes ready to be the first to "tell" when the agenda starts:

1. "The best moment I remember with my father was when. . . ." [Make it a description of an event, complete with details, actual words spoken, gestures made—everything.]

2. "When I look in the mirror, the things I see that are most like my father are. . . ."

3. "If I could 'replay' my childhood with my father, if I could change one thing, it would be. . . ."

4. Do a group recitation—eyes open—of the Lord's Prayer. Now tell what comes to mind when you said "Our Father. . . ."

Huddle up, circling and enveloping each other in solid masculine ways for closing prayer and the pledge of ongoing commitment to each other's stories, journeys, and new construction.

CHAPTER THREE

DEFAULT: HI MOM!

One of the most remarkable women I ever met was Julia Shelhamer. She was a legend by the time I was fifteen, when I read her husband's amazing book *Heart Talks for Boys.* Julia's name appeared on the volume, *Heart Talks for Girls.* I first met Julia when she moved to Winona Lake, Indiana. She would have been in her eighties.

Julia was a veteran of street rescue mission operations in Shreveport, Louisiana, and Washington, D.C. So when she first arrived at Winona Lake, Indiana, she was under-employed in an all-white Christian resort center with two denominational headquarters surrounding her. One of my colleagues happened on to her cosmic loneliness when he asked how she enjoyed living at Winona Lake.

Julia's instant reply shocked him, "Very well, but I miss the drunks." So Julia embarked on a career of visiting bars and cocktail lounges in Kosciusko County and surrounding counties—always on Thursday afternoons. I asked her once, since my wildest imagination could not picture this little old evangelist of a woman in a bar, "What do you do when you visit the cocktail lounges and bars?"

"Oh, Mr. Joy," she said, "you know that three of us older women go every Thursday afternoon. But younger women couldn't do what we do. I always ask the proprieter whether I can speak to his patrons, of course. And I have never been refused. Then I approach some man who is sitting all alone. I sit down near him. When he looks at me, I say to him, 'Do you have a mother?' "

"Tell me about your mother," opens one of the most important windows into any person's life. And it may be that sons are more attached to their mothers than daughters are. I have asked myself this question when I see consistent signals in our culture of this special relationship: What is it that motivates NFL players to wave greetings to their mothers when the television cameras play on them? I've found myself speculating: *Are these men without fathers?* Or is there a special link between a young man and his mother that accounts for the universal "Hi Mom!" as he gazes into a TV camera?

In *Bonding: Relationships in the Image of God,* I speculate about the curious breaking-away rituals which girls practice to establish autonomy from their mothers. But even more visible, in the standard two-parent family, are boys turning to their mothers as they launch into manhood. At that same time they become relatively distant toward their fathers, as if to enter into the adult domain by themselves.

MOTHER'S GIFT

The bond between a birth mother and her child is unique, of course. The universal bonding principle that motivates mothers of all warm-blooded species to give constant and effective care and protection to the newly born or hatched is a miracle. Without it, the infant mortality rate would quickly wipe out most species.

We know in humans, for example, that vaginally delivered babies are so stressed by travel through the birth canal that they literally arrive with a brain-released chemical high which causes them to spend up to at least their first three hours wide awake. During these hours birth bonding tends to cement them to the mother's visual image, unique odors, and voice. Now that physicians are arranging for birthing training for fathers and are bringing them like Joseph with Mary into the birthing chambers, the same powerful bonds can be established between father and infant. Indeed, fathers who give that first care while the mother is recovering from an unusually troublesome delivery, often find that their children continue to run for their arms when they need special care or comfort. In such cases the mother may feel rejected by such a spontaneous and lifelong pattern of primary dependency on the male. But the pattern remains strong because it is rooted in the hours immediately following birth.

Mothers, compared to fathers, simply by their own preference and by the opportunities afforded them in most cultures, spend more time with young children. Mothers are the center of attachment for most of us. We depend on them to be there, to provide food, and to comfort us. Mothers know us in a literal and naked sense. To look into Mother's face is to realize that there is no place to hide from her: she knows us from the beginning.

For nearly twenty years I have sent my graduate students to tell stories to children and elicit moral judgments from them about ways to fix things that have gone wrong. We often add some abstract questions after the stories. One of the more interesting sets of responses comes when an interviewer asks, "Do you think God is more like a father or more like a mother?" And since we are replicating moral reasoning in these anecdotal interviews, we steel ourselves against correcting their answers. My students have found that boys under ten years old often say that God is more like a mother than a father.

"Why do you think God is more like a mother?" has to be the next question. Look at the logic and the concrete reality of the explanations we typically get: "Because He takes care of you." "God won't let you go hungry." "You can always come back when you've done something bad or run away That's the way it is with mothers."

When Mother is the birth mother, she is literally the source of life. The "seed of the woman" leaves its genetic marker across the generations in a way that father's seed does not. So while most of us carry our father's names, we also carry the genetic marker in our mitochondrial DNA, by which we can be linked across all our generations to all of our mothers, even to the first Mother. All living humans, researchers now have discovered, show mitochondrial DNA linkage back to one common mother of us all.[1]

MOTHER'S WARMTH

The origin of life occurs within the body of the mother, so it is easy to trace the child's magnetic pull toward her as the center of warmth—literally the oven of primal life. Add to that the happy effects of intimate contact in the early hours and years of life, and it is easy to see that life's surest security is deposited with Mother!

The affectional center of a family tends to rest, also, in Mother. I am intrigued by the rich metaphors of the Creation narrative in Genesis. Among those pictures which are worth contemplating is that of the woman being built up from the parts of Adam drawn from the *tsela* or *pleura,* literally the thorasic cavity.

The Hebrew word *tsela,* commonly translated "rib," is a construction term, not an anatomic word and refers to the vertical pieces of the interior of the hull of a wooden boat— the ribs. So, when the chest cavity is opened, our ribs show through as vertical "studdings" around which the body is stretched like the outer "skin" of a boat. It is easy to expand the surgical imagery of Creation to see why the Hebrew *tsela* was translated *pleura* in the Greek translation of the Old Testament. We get our medical term *pleurisy* from *pleura.* Both *tsela* and *pleura* evoke images of the entire thorasic cavity opened, much as modern open-heart surgery separates the rib cage at the sternum and goes into the life center of our body. According to Genesis 2, woman is formed from this "heart," this affectional center of the original Adam.[2]

The heart denotes the center of affections and beliefs in biblical imagery; the opening of the center of Adam was likely intended to give us a picture of mother as one created out of the most affectional resources present in Adam—the undifferentiated, unsplit totally human being. Research has validated this point, for women, taken as a group, consistently score higher than men on affective and affectional measures. Isabel Briggs Myers found, when she validated her now famous Myers-Briggs Personality Inventory, that sex differences appeared only in one pair of poles in her four sets: 60 percent of women compared to 40 percent of men showed a preference for making decisions based on "feeling," or the "human considerations" involved. Just the opposite pattern showed for "thinking," or "pure, rational, factual decision-making": men, 60 percent and women, 40 percent. On all other scales men and women were evenly divided. Remember that women's brains combine both feelings and reasoning, while men are often "single-minded."[3]

With this sex difference, we see how sons might find this "opposite" characteristic in Mother to be a powerful magnet. Being placed between a rational father and an affectional mother guarantees a child will be aware of the full spectrum of environment in which he has been formed. And the tendency for opposites to attract may be another reason why sons tend to depend on mothers.

The opposite magnet provides the clue to mothers' powerful attachment to their sons. Likewise, so desperate is the yearning of a young woman for male affirmation that one of the most pronounced effects of father absence for her shows up in the search for a man. This pilgrimage, which sets out to replace the missing father in her life, often leads her to premature sexual adventures and pregnancy. But the startling bottom line of her search consistently shows up in the research on father absence, in the illegitimate birthrate, and in decisions to keep the baby. That bottom line consideration is reduced to a logical syllogism in the mind of a girl who feels abandoned by her father. It is simply this:

1. If I cannot have Daddy, I will find myself a man.

2. Any man will do, since I am so worthless that Daddy left, and I cannot therefore expect to find a really good man.

3. If I get pregnant by a man, maybe he will marry me.

4. Even if he does not marry me, if I can have a baby, maybe it will be a boy. Then I will raise me a man.

In chapter 1, I summarized the profound difference between male and female brain organization. To the extent that a son suffers from that male single-mindedness, which tends to keep his affective right hemisphere from translating easily into the speech produced in his left hemisphere, it is likely Mother who best can read and articulate the boy's true feelings. Deprived of easy access to putting their feelings into words, boys may find it easier to ventilate those nonspeech expressions of emotions in Mother's presence. The tears, the sighs, and surrender of anger—all of these will be understood by Mother. Mother is the safe haven of affection, and no taboos exist in the Western world against a boy of any age who wants to hug his mother, hold her, or cry on her shoulder.

Daddy, in the eyes of the son, is more likely in his single-minded view of the world to either put logical solutions in place, give advice, or to simply ventilate emotions through nonlinguistic expressions such as profanity or gestures of violence. None of these reactions are particularly attractive to young boys, so it is to Mother's comfort that they flee.

The "default" back to Mother and away from a developing masculinity locks many young men into perpetual boyhood, into the Peter Pan swing of a forever childhood. So it will be important for the young man to see his mother as a source of affirmation, as "the other" compared to himself and his father. She holds mysterious empowerment in her ways of mothering him to launch him well.

MOTHER'S POLISH

Let me replay a scenario that is almost universal. Try to figure out what is going on.

My son is going through my shaving gear in the master bathroom. I hear a shout, "Daddy! Can you come help me for a minute?"

I go only to find that he has my electric razor out. He has already removed the darkening hair above his lip and has squared off the teardrop sideburns that have been forming now for several weeks as the promise of real whiskers. All of that hair growth is gone. He has figured out the razor perfectly. After all, I had to give him a first turn at the age of two when he toddled in every morning during my shave, hoping that I would let him be a little man. After a few seconds of feeling the vibration of the back of the razor applied to his cheek, he was satisfied, his male sex role batteries charged for the day.

"Where is your shaving lotion—the kind you always use? I couldn't find it," he anxiously inquires.

I don't know how he missed that part of the secret male formula. No matter, I go into the lower section of the storage unit and retrieve the Brut. He takes over, and I leave him to apply my favorite scent—regularly supplied by his mother on my birthdays. I offer him the facial talcum too, though I seldom bother to use it.

All is silent for a few minutes, then Mr. Handsome appears, ready for an important evening out. He looks like a million dollars, right down to his latest clothing, handpicked to his own taste. As he comes across the family room I notice an uneasy look on his face. I rise to praise him and see him off, but in his intensity, he charges past me and into the kitchen.

"How do I look, Mom? I'm ready." He is cautious with her. *Is he afraid of her response?* I wonder. His words are spoken softly as if they may be the last words he will ever speak, unless her response is one that will refuel his empty tank.

"Wow," she whispers. "I can't believe it, yet here it is: My son, The Man! He is tall. He is handsome. And he even has the smell of a man on him. What ever happened to my baby boy?" She hugs him, kissing him lightly on the cheek, then holds him at arm's length for a second look.

Imagine such a thing. Here I sit with the evening paper in my lap. I was good enough to provide the razor and to lay out the Brut. But who does he run to for an appraisal? His mother. What does she know about manhood?

It would be easy to extend the scenario of self-pity and rejection, and to end up in an explosion of anger which would drive alienation deep in all of our relationships. If that happens, the father is marginalized, and the "mother-son" dyad becomes a competitive threat to the marriage. But the scene I have described is virtually never an expression of mother-son fixation or an alternative to marital attachment. Instead, the boy simply needs an authoritative judgment on his masculinity and marketability as a man, so he turns to the consumer professional—to his mother, who has picked Dad out of a crowd and is a connoisseur of "good manhood" credentials.

Seen in this light, the boy's presentation to his mother is the highest compliment he can pay his father. It is as if the son is saying, "Mom, look me over. Am I as well put together as Dad was when you first met him? Am I as good looking? Do I smell right? Do I pass your judgment? You were the one who picked Dad and I have imitated and admired him since I was born. Do I measure up?"

Mothers do the "final polish" for sons, who growing up admiring their dads, have imitated every small detail of gender-appropriate behavior, right down to vocabulary and manner of walking. Dads furnish the same mirror for their daughters. Healthy teen and young adult women have fathers who admire and affirm them. Such women glow with a sense of wellness, defined by Daddy's words and the knowledge that he would die for their safety and well-being. In this way the image of God invested in the father-mother unit emerges again, faithful to sons and daughters who need the final touch of affirmation to launch them as healthy women and men.

MOTHER'S LOVE

What is the core of personality? What are the core character components in men and women? At Harvard's Center for the Study of Moral Development, Lawrence Kohlberg, in an important career cut short by his untimely death, reported exactly what Jean Piaget had found working with children in Switzerland: Justice is the core of human character, and it is universal across the cultures. Justice, it turns out, begins with concern for the self, a cry for fairness. But as it unfolds in later childhood and into maturity, a healthy person applies the fairness rule to other people, eventually to all people, and a more complicated commitment to equality and equity appears.

Kohlberg and Piaget worked almost exclusively with boys. Carol Gilligan, a Kohlberg student later turned colleague, courageously asked whether justice was indeed the core for women's moral judgment as well. Her findings? Women are more complicated in "moral reasoning" and make their judgments on other issues more complex than simple justice. That moral base is "attachment." Women tend to become seriously involved in moral decision making—involved with the complicated "people dimensions," how people are affected, how they feel. So urgent is the need to reach out that they are unable to stand outside of a problem. Instead, they must solve problems while remaining intimately connected to all of the participants—no matter how polarized they may be from one another. Gilligan found the moral development of girls and women to parallel the unfolding justice structure in the classical research on boys and men, but female judgments are profoundly more subjective and complex than the calculating objective decisions of men.[4]

This gift of attachment is an important balance to the more objective sense of justice which is required for minimum law and order in any human community. But the complementary balance of justice and love provides more than a self-correcting set of principles for society: A mother and a father bring balancing moral gifts to the world of the developing child. What a child experiences as "mother's love" and as "father's fairness" are the ultimate balanced scale of God's image offered to children.

When we think of Mother's love, it is easy to become nostalgic and sentimental. Sweet as our memories might be, they fail to touch upon our larger needs. If a woman's moral sense is "completing" to a man's sense of justice, then we must place women along with men in every arena where moral decisions and counsel are on the agenda—in the community, in the church, in the state and nation.

The roots of Mother's attachment gift and of Father's justice perspective are most clearly traced in the doctrine of

Creation. The "image of God" is distributed to and reflected in humanity as male and female. At its best, the sovereign, "wholly-otherness" of God's righteousness is imaged by the universal tendency of men to stand outside of events and to make cool, objective judgments. On the other hand, women tend to represent God's other side by embracing the world with unconditional love and attachment, and meting out judgments that take into account the subjective concerns of all participants.

At their worst, men tend to make cold, insensitive judgments and become trapped victims of "the facts." Super-rational men, often oblivious to the human dimensions of their world, tend to knuckle under as workaholics, and serve as indentured slaves of analytic careers and of machines.

And at their worst, women become emotionally attached to too many people. They may be seduced into nearly fatal compromises, sometimes unable to decide because the dilemmas are too complex. Such women often fall victim to mental overload, emotional paralysis, or psychological disorders. Their faltering cry of failure is that of the first woman, "I was deceived."

It is clear that the "Mother Love" and "Father Justice" gifts are self-correcting where both are present, fully charged, and attentive to each other. The fully functional monogamous family in multiple generations, then, is certainly the ideal environment in which to be formed as a healthy and balanced human.

MOTHER'S SUPERVISION

The mother-child attachment establishes the potential bond within which the child grows to responsible adulthood. Father-bonding, such as Joseph's providential role in Jesus' delivery, or as it is intentionally arranged in hospitals today, can provide parallel foundations for high quality attachment between father and child from infancy across a lifetime.

There is no better predictor of children's "risk" for compulsive addiction to alcohol, sex, and drugs than to look at their family system. I unfold four typical family systems in my book, *Parents, Kids, and Sexual Integrity*. A high quality father-mother relationship is the single best predictor of the healthy and risk-proof child.[5]

One of the most intriguing family systems studies ever completed is rarely mentioned today. Yet the work of two Harvard Law School professors, published in 1950, under the title, *Unraveling Juvenile Delinquency*, was a comprehensive and carefully done study. Its accuracy for predicting households with potentially healthy or potentially criminal boys is unrivaled. Today, we badly need a replication of the Sheldon and Eleanor Glueck study, both to bring it up to date and to extend it to the female population as well.

The Gluecks, weary of training law students whose energies would be consumed by large logs of adolescent criminal cases, set about to study the characteristics of delinquents— then almost exclusively boys. They were eager to unravel the causes of delinquency, in the hope that by knowing its sources, all of us could help prevent it. By "juvenile delinquency," the Gluecks referred to criminal convictions of juveniles, who if they had been of legal age as adults, would have been prosecuted for misdemeanor or felony convictions.

The Gluecks began by identifying 500 persistent delinquent boys and 500 nondelinquent boys who were matched by age, intelligence, ethnic derivation, and neighborhood conditions. The 1,000 boys were studied on more than 400 traits and factors. The researchers looked for anything which consistently correlated with delinquency or non-delinquency. From the 120 social factors in family backgrounds, five factors emerged which accurately correlated with delinquency and non-delinquency—at opposite ends of the spectrums on each of the 5 factors:

1. Discipline of the boy by the father
2. Discipline of the boy by the mother
3. Affection of the father for the boy
4. Affection of the mother for the boy
5. Cohesiveness of the family.

In 1952, the New York City Youth Board (NYCYB) began the first follow-up of young children to test the reliability of the Glueck social prediction table. They selected 303 boys, ages five and six, of white, black, Jewish, and Puerto Rican descent, and followed them for ten years. Since many of the boys came from mother-only homes, Maude M. Craig and Selma J. Glick modified the Glueck five-point factors, reducing them to:

1. Discipline of the boy by mother or mother substitute
2. Supervision of the boy by the mother
3. Cohesiveness of the family unit.

Craig and Glick developed some technical definitions. "Suitable discipline" referred to parental correction that was reasonable and explained to the boy. It might include physical consequences, loss of privileges, and other common parent-child disciplines. The mother was consistent, verbal, and reasonable. "Unsuitable discipline" included "no discipline at all," along with inconsistent, unreasonable, punitive, overly strict punishment for the slightest infraction of the mother's rules.

"Suitable supervision" included an agreement between mother and child that she must always know where the boy was and with whom he was associated. She needed to know his friends. If she worked outside the home, the boy must be in the care of an adult who was equally committed to the boy's welfare. "Unsuitable supervision" included only partial knowledge about the boy, inconsistent attention to his welfare, and even emotional and physical abandonment.

"Cohesiveness in the family" was characterized by an atmosphere of affection and mutual dependence among family members. The boy found the home to be his important place of security and belongingness. Family celebrations were like clockwork, and meals brought the family together daily. The "unintegrated home," at the extreme delinquent end, was marked by the extreme self-interest of all family members — the house was a place to sleep. Meals were erratic and unpredictable, and virtually no attention was given to family celebrations.

Using those three factors and intermediate points in between the poles I have summarized here, the NYCYB across a ten-year span revisited the boys when they were fifteen and sixteen years old. They lost track of only one of the 303 boys in the sample. The results of the tracking for ten years were most astounding! Look at the Glueck proof that these three factors actually predicted a boy's future moral behavior:

97.1 percent accuracy in predicting non-delinquency.

84.8 percent accuracy in predicting delinquency.[6]

Ken Magid, in his terrifying 1987 book, *High Risk,*[7] reminds us that the lack of family bonding is presenting North America with such seriously damaged children that the entire culture is at risk. These potentially destructive, damaged children now coming in sizeable numbers into the adult population are an increasing worry. Given the economic reality of "two incomes" as the minimum basis on which to buy a home and launch a family, many parents have put their children into the high-risk pool. They will likely have made that decision by default, seeing their standard of living as more important than the stable environment they might have provided by investing fewer prime hours in the workplace. And the single parent, under so many stresses already, surely has a gigantic task in maintaining order and stability in the non-traditional household.

But the sign of peace and hope is clear: Mother's discipline, supervision, and structuring of family life, even for the single-parent home, might leverage a 97.1 percent probability that the kids will not be teenage felons.

IN SEARCH OF MOTHER

We have no studies of mother absence to compare the likely effects on either sons or daughters. The father absence studies were begun following World War II, and established the effects on both sons and daughters. Eventually we found that those painful effects varied in predictable ways depending on other factors:

1. How early the loss occurred.

2. Why the father disappeared from the child's world.

Today, with the increasing cases of mother abandonment, and the significant number of single-parent homes headed by males, we deserve to know more clearly what those predictable mother-absence effects might be. To inform our questions we might expect that chldren without mothers would suffer deprivation at obvious levels: affectional development, security, self-esteem, and confidence in their sex-role development.

Many years ago now, I was intrigued with the central mother theme in Hermann Hesse's novel, *Narcissus and Goldmund.* In the story, young Goldmund is delivered to the monastic cloister by his father. When the senior priest reports to the faculty that the boy has no brothers or sisters, and no mother, he urges them to be a father to the boy to make up for his homesickness.

But Narcissus, a young teaching-monk, watches Goldmund flower from childhood into young manhood at eighteen. Narcissus reports to the Abbot that Goldmund suffers because he has forgotten a part of his past—his mother, and all connected with her.

The Abbot recalls that there may be a reason for the forgetting, and without telling Narcissus his thoughts, remembers that Goldmund's father had reported that his wife had abandoned them, run away when the boy was young, and brought shame upon them both. The father had tried to suppress the mother's memory in the boy. The Abbot speculated that he had succeeded, inasmuch as Goldmund gave up his life to God as an atonement for his mother's sins.

Without help from the Abbot, Narcissus eventually supports the depressed and failing Goldmund in his desire to leave school and go in search of his own world. Most of the novel traces the playboy's search for love, his using and being used by women. Occasionally he returns to visit the cloister and to bring Narcissus up to date on his misadventures. After many years, Goldmund, fearfully ill and actually dying, returns to Narcissus. He has, by this time, established a fine reputation as a woodcarver who specializes in sanctuary images. His major unfinished piece is Eve—the original Mother.

The closing days of Goldmund's life find him opening up the hidden memories of his mother. "Do you remember?" he asks Narcissus. "I had completely forgotten my mother until you conjured her up again." The powerful novel ends with Narcissus—the man who truly understood Goldmund, and who read humanity as if it were an open book—receiving Goldmund's final confession.

"I cannot wait until tomorrow. I must say farewell to you now, and as we part I must tell you everything. Listen to me another moment. I wanted to tell you about my mother, and how she keeps her fingers clasped around my heart...."

So Goldmund unfolds the summary of his quest and of his regret that the Eve figure is unfinished. "Only a short while ago it would have been unbearable to me to think that I might die without having carved her statue; my life would have seemed useless to me. And now see how strangely things have turned out: It is not my hands that shape and form her; it is her hands that shape and form me."

Having "studied" women for his entire adult life, he has been trying to portray all of womanhood and of all mothers in his image of Eve.

"I can still see it, and if I had force in my hands, I could carve it. But she doesn't want that; she doesn't want me to make her secret visible," Goldmund explains.

Narcissus is deeply shaken by the confession and the revelation. Goldmund had known something about Narcissus that caught him off guard. Finally, the dying man opened his eyes, saying farewell without words. Then, suddenly, gathering all of his energy for a final question, he whispers, "But how will you die when your time comes, Narcissus, since you have no mother? Without a mother, one cannot love. Without a mother, one cannot die."[8]

Hesse's tale marks men well. Indeed, all men are born of women, and unfinished business between a man and his mother is at the root of much of the secret agony and unspeakable secrets hidden deep inside of men. The ultimate "default" is a man who uses women, abuses women, and devalues women because his mother work was badly botched.

 # Do-It-Yourself Tips

Try a mirror talk now with mother issues. The eyes: are they hers? the facial structure? the lips? Check yourself out—where are the visible genetic marks of your mother?

1. Recall the most blessed episode in your young career—what did she say or do that turned you into a competent young man? Let the memory play through the years and return the blessing to her. Pick up words she said and say them again to yourself, now.

2. Be in touch with her today—a call, a card, a note celebrating her launching you so well.

3. If you have lost your mother to death or in any other way, look again deeply into your own eyes. Give yourself permission to grieve. Bless the gifts she gave to your aspiring manhood, even the fragments if there wasn't much.

Contractor's Crew Notes

Tighten down the superficial "man talk" as your group settles in, and open it with these stems on which you have done your own preparation:

1. "The best memory I have of my relationship with my mother is when...."

2. "If I could replay just one day of my early life with my mother and have it come out differently, it would be when...."

3. "I remember drawing some of my early manly strength from another woman who was like a second mother to me. The way she blessed me was...."

Huddle for your group affirmation, sealing your stories into each others' keeping and supporting each other in prayer.

CHAPTER FOUR

DISORIENTATION: IN SEARCH OF SELF?

Ray obviously started out large for his age. Big-boned, tall, and lean as an adult, it was easy to believe his description of the early years.

"When I started to kindergarten the teacher took me aside and appealed to me to help her watch after this kid with severe problems. She had me figured out. I was your compliant child, wanting to please everybody, but especially adults. It was like they thought I was volunteering to be the teacher's helper. The same thing happened every year. I can name the kids I got assigned to. And I took it so seriously that I never did get to play or work with the ordinary kids. I was always 'baby-sitting' somebody with a big problem. I never complained."

Ray went on, "When I look at my class pictures from elementary school, I can see why they did it to me. I would have done it to myself. For example, in my second grade class picture I was as big as the teacher. There we stand. I am on the left end of the picture and she is on the right end. And in between the two of us are all these normal little kids."

We were looking for the roots to Ray's adult loneliness and his lifetime of essentially being without people who were close to him. "When I hit seventh grade I discovered basketball, so I knew it was a good option coming into junior high school. And I was good. I was so good that I got to play with older players, and performed competitively from seventh grade on. That gave me status, prestige, and recognition from my peers. But I didn't know how to relate to them any other way. It was very safe to earn my social points in basketball competition; I only had to deal with the applause. Off the court I wanted to hide. I simply didn't want to be around people. I felt clumsy and shy, yet I needed to be close to people."

It was clear. Ray's underdeveloped social skills complicated the people dimension of his life at a very critical season of development. In this chapter, I want to walk you through a sequence of agendas boys and men face in the journey toward healthy adulthood.

BECOMING A MAN: MARKERS ON THE JOURNEY

The first rule about humans we see in the Creation account is that it is "not good that we should be alone." Indeed, becoming human requires substantial social contact. Let's look at several specific areas:

Parental bonding and meeting needs. Chapters 2 and 3 unfold detailed ways in which "fathering" and "mothering" are crucial shaping forces in the life of a boy. I have written books targeted to my teenage grandsons and granddaughters which gently unwrap my best hopes for them. *Becoming a Man*[1] and *Celebrating the New Woman*[2] are my best statements about how families meet the needs of the emerging young adults in their households. I much prefer to spin out "best case scenarios."

In his book, *High Risk,* Ken Magid and his colleague Carol McKelvey caution about predictable effects of non-bonded children. They suggest two factors which must be addressed in the first twenty-four months of life. If we do not "catch the tide" during these months, the effects tend to leave lifelong tracks and become core agendas for the growing child.

At least 50 percent of a person's total, lifelong learning, Magid and McKelvey insist, comes during the first year of life. The next 25 percent is in place by the end of the second year. All of us beyond age two are simply "topping off" the basic life-orientation of "meaning making" laid down in the first twenty-four months.

Every adult's sense of security and optimism — basic trust toward the universe — is laid down in what Magid calls the critical first year's "bonding cycle" of the responsive infant. Magid diagrams the bonding cycle to show that if (1) the infant child's NEED is followed by (2) its RAGE REACTION in the absence of speech, there must follow (3) GRATIFICATION or RELIEF of the need, met by an adult. This leads to (4) TRUST — the reassuring sense that "When I am in need, an answer to my need is already on the way." High quality child-care centers work hard to create that predictable "need-meeting" environment, but without a nurturing, bonded one-on-one caregiver on board, the critical first years may leave scars of insecurity and shame-like feelings of worthlessness.[3]

Early social contact. A full spectrum of social skills involving people older, younger, and the same age develops only if the child has a full spectrum of early social contact. If, for example, a child is four years old, he or she needs to spend an average of four hours each day with peers. The age-mate formula calls for "as many hours each day in social contact with peers as matches the 'year' age of the child." The only child, or oldest child whose siblings do not arrive for several years, tends to develop good skills with adults, but less effective ones with age-mates.

Same-sex confidential friendships. It was Paul Tournier's book *Secrets* which gave me my first conscious "wake-up call" about children's ripening need to share their secrets with friends. Tournier reported that children by school age must have privacy in order to develop "individuality." Then, during transition into adolescence, the child begins to share these secrets. This may involve opening the locked box or digging through the private drawer in the presence of one or two trusted same-sex friends. This sharing of secrets includes verbal secrets, shared personal experiences, questions, fears, and violation of taboos. To the axiom, "Best friends know," we can easily add, "Best friends never tell."

Here, upon spilling one's secrets, Tournier reminds us, the individual is transformed into a person, because in this Christian psychiatrist's view, people always become a person in relation to others. Tournier describes how the confidential friendships of teenage years are preparation for the exclusive, lifelong covenant we enter into in a one-flesh, one-mind marriage. For it is only in marriage that we are loved and "known as we are known" in "ultimate naked honesty."[4]

Hetero-social competence. For several years now, I have been intentionally listening for clues about Tournier's agenda of privacy and shared secrets as they relate to high quality monogamous dating and marriage. The strength of a marriage is directly related to the degree of honesty in the relationship. So, I speculated that "telling the truth" to each other was something all of us had learned before we approached marriage.

When Manny signed up for an appointment on a university campus where I was a visiting lecturer, I was startled at his youthfulness.

"How old are you?" I began.

"Sixteen."

"How do you get to be a college freshman at sixteen?"

"My parents were missionaries, so I did a lot of my work by homeschooling. But I want to talk about the loneliness I feel around here. Someday I'm sure I'll be ready for bonding, and all of those things you write and talk about, but right now I need a guy friend. Yet most guys seem to avoid me when they see how much I need them. Am I weird or something?"

I listened carefully to Manny's primal cry for friendship. Yes, he said, there was one guy in orchestra that he really wanted to be close to. But then he admitted a problem: "He's dating, and I can't ask him to spend time with me. It wouldn't be right to cut in on them."

I couldn't get his age off my mind, and Paul Tournier's time line of privacy followed by confidential sharing clicked. So I pressed him for a bit of history. Where had he lived and how many schools had he attended between the age of ten and now? The answer was shocking: four middle schools in three years, then another move and the high school turned out to be plagued by violence, so his parents ordered in Accelerated Christian Education curriculum which he completed in two years to arrive here at age sixteen. Manny was essentially locked away from peer contact during the "tide of needs" years, and starved for significant friendship at a time when male development suffers profoundly if held in a vacuum. Critical social skills and deep social yearnings had been put on hold. We wound up our appointment time with a game plan to bring three guys, not one, into a fellowship group that would include daily meals in the campus cafeteria and weekend activities together. Manny made an appointment with the dean of students to see whether the group could be pulled into a recovery network actually supervised by that office. It is not uncommon for young men with empty spots in their peer network during early adolescence to suffer deeply from feelings of social isolation and frustration. And for this reason alone, many of them label themselves and are labeled homosexual, yet their innocent need has been "homo-social" rehearsal for "hetero-social" competence which follows.

I remembered, too, Harry Harlow's famous studies with rhesus monkeys. He discovered that peer friendship appears to be very important for adolescent primates. He gave names to a half dozen or more specific characteristics of peer love. In his tape series, *Speaking of Love*[5], Harlow observes, with a bit of sadness, that we have no words to describe a similar human need practiced on the way to maturity. The way in which young girls depend on other girls, and young boys on other boys, for serious and supportive friendship is a critical developmental stage among humans that reflects Harlow's primates discoveries. To be deprived of peer friendship is to be deformed as an adult.

So, in the fall of 1991, I offered my three lunch-hour support groups the challenge of reconstructing our confidential friendship networks beginning at the age of ten. We developed a set of symbols to use in chalkboard sketches of those middle-school, high-school, and remaining years of our lives. The stories were amazingly good "history giving" foundations for our work together on other issues, but such a spectrum ranging from rich fulfillment to utter isolation I never expected to hear!

Everyone also completed a 32-item anonymous questionnaire which chronicled the degree to which same-sex friendships were important to us during our early years, the college years, and our present graduate school experience. When I separated the unmarried from the married men's data, here are the unusual patterns which emerged. Using "10" as "very true of me" and "1" as "not at all," the numbers show the increasing importance of "same-sex confidential friendships" across a couple of decades or more of life:

Confidential, High-Trust Male Friendships Rated on 10-Point Scale of Importance

	Singles	Marrieds
Middle School Years	3.8	4.7
High School Years	4.2	7.8
College/University Years	7.0	7.3
Graduate School/Seminary Years	8.6*	7.7

*Note that the data were collected in all-male support network groups during the graduate school/seminary career and may overrepresent singles now committed to "catch up" their deficit of male bonding experiences.

There is an obvious correlation between early male confidential-trust friendships and earlier marriage. But it is equally clear that those early priorities on male friendships continue with the married men across the decades. You can also speculate that single males — 40 percent of the total respondents — are giving themselves permission in the graduate school years to try to "catch the tide" that passed them in middle school.

Our stories, shared across an entire semester, were stunning in many ways. Men who felt isolated, marginalized, and lonely during middle school *never* remembered being successful in establishing confidential male friendships during the high school years. High school, it turned out, was remembered as a time of high social anxiety, or superficiality, or being afraid to tell anyone what they really felt or worried about. Their secrets were frozen unless they had brought middle school confidants into pubescence. But the university years tended to be the "breakthrough" time in their remembered social experience. Breaking away from home, they frequently found confidential, trustworthy male friends. We heard the spectrum which spanned from high-trust friends found around a common commitment to Jesus and to maintaining faith during the university years, all the way to the naked emotional honesty of rebellious partners who found solidarity in their fast-lane destructive lifestyles.

You can imagine that we pondered the foundational usefulness of same-sex confidential, high-trust friendships as a credential for the helping professions and for Christian pastoral ministry, in particular. But a major reflection came as we realized that children isolated from peers during middle school deserve special attention in the life of a congregation and that parents are often the catalysts of social development for their children. Overnights, recreational programs, and church youth ministries are vital arenas beyond the schools in which young people may make the confidential friends they so much need before trying their wings in hetero-social dating and pursuit of love and marriage.

NURTURING MALENESS AND MASCULINITY

Garth, age eight, blurted out the excitement of having found a new girlfriend. The family, in the middle of the evening meal, burst into a mockery of Garth's innocent but urgent information. He never again shared his "best news," and, indeed, drove his attraction for girls underground. He blushed and felt ashamed whenever feelings of love and attraction stirred within. I met him twenty years later when he shared his story of inappropriate sexual behavior, one that continued to plague him into young adulthood.

Boys are profoundly more fragile in their sense of sexual identity and sex-appropriate behavior than are girls. In chapter 1 I outlined the sequence of development by which a basically "female" fetus is modified into a male as a boy is brought into the world. Since the standard model of genital and brain formation, including sexual orientation in the brain, is the female model, heterosexually oriented males are a profoundly modified variation from that female brain.

Powerful male hormones, androgens, do their part in developing the male. The mother's supply of them accomplishes the male genital transformation. And the little male fetus does his part in providing a tiny trickle of androgens, including some of the mighty testosterone, by the twelfth or thirteenth week of development as the testicles begin their performance.

Again at pubescence, the massive charges of male hormones arising out of the boy's sex system provide compelling demands and matching energy to pull the young male toward a sexually differentiated body build with masculine body hair patterns. The hormonal surge of pubescence is a powerful motor to drive him toward finding sexual outlet and pleasure.

During the critical early adolescent years it is crucial that a young man's sexual energy be irrevocably connected to his feelings and affections. Yet these are the years when sexual exploitation in this culture tries to seduce him into sex for "kicks," for competition, or reward—apart from affection and lifelong bonding.

If his social "rights" of scoring as a self-reward for athletic or other achievement do not move him to premature sexual activity, even the most isolated young man remains a sitting duck for the sex marketeers. He may be drawn into using the *Playboy* centerfold as a masturbation stimulus. He may be enticed into trying the sexual services marketed at an adult bookstore, or be seduced or partied into exchanging sexual pleasures with acquaintances. These are also the years when a young man's sexual energy easily laminates itself to sexually explicit language, four-letter words, and obscenities in general. To the extent that these violent and impersonal stimuli come early and consistently in a young man's life they may create a lifetime attraction to such impersonal and artificial experience, whether they be on paper, in film, or part of the imagination. When they do, lifelong marital bonding is profoundly put at risk, and sexual addictions that will plague him for decades are easily put in place.

Family affirmation of the young awakening male is crucial. It is important to nurture his capacity for friendship and to bolster his confidence in his budding masculinity. If we are intentional about it, we will find appropriate opportunities to give him positive feedback. He needs to know that he is attractive and that we are ready to empower and launch him in his own time as a fine husband and father. These are the real markers of adult status and value as a male, yet they lie out of reach of many teenage boys. And good families frequently frustrate and deny their sons, leaving them to imagine that the tough economic times doom them to lives of celibacy or of promiscuity and premarital infidelity.

Sexual identity is not an automatic gift of biology. By sexual identity I refer to the interior sense of a person's judgments about himself: I am a male. "Sex role" refers to the way a man packages himself to present to the outer world. Occasionally a "macho" male is hollow, sensing in his "inner world" that he is not secure as a male—so he "cross dresses" between his real interior "sexual identity" and his publicly presented "sex role." The transvestite is not the only "cross dresser" around.

Our "sexual identity" is constructed from a thousand pieces of "meaning" which we weave into a coherent self-image. Parental statements, protection, naming, and behavior will have given every child most of the "content" to weave into "sexual identity." But we also weave in our own feelings, our own perceptions about our bodies, our emotions, and our sensations. From these conglomerated perceptions, each of us will make sexual identity conclusions about ourselves. We will either make judgments affirming ourselves or else will raise uneasy questions about our sexuality: I sometimes wonder whether I am OK as a male?

Sexual identity is largely constructed from perceptions we collect from the significant people in our lives. Parents, grandparents, siblings, and friends of the family all play strategic roles. Those people not only provide a million verbal and nonverbal "statements" about how they see the child, they also furnish specific feedback on the boy's sex-appropriate behavior.

Gary's father tacked the nickname of "Fairy" onto an angelically blond and introverted little boy. It took Gary to age thirty to shake loose from the homosexual innuendo of his father's crude label. His father evidently based the label on the small-boned, fragile looking structure of the little toddler. What seemed like a game to an often drunken father became a damaging and crippling "sexual identity" for Gary as he made his way through pubescence with the public shame of the community nickname.

When a family friend, trusted perhaps more than any other, and perhaps motivated by the "Fairy" nickname, seduced sixteen-year-old Gary into a single homosexual experience, the label became a tangible "experienced based" albatross around his neck. But as a father of two children, deeply devoted to his wife and with no trace of homosexual preference, it became important for Gary to reconstruct his sexual identity from the very earliest days. This was accomplished in the protective atmosphere of one of our nurturing groups.

In a sex-crazed and often confused culture, it is clear that certain guidelines must be followed to furnish positive perceptual data to boys as they try to make sense of their own sexual identity. Let me suggest a few:

1. Make it priority to give young boys significant time and access to the important man in their lives. If Dad is not always available, place the child in close proximity to significant male relatives, or surrogate father options. Churches with a strong sense of community can often provide such supplementary "Dad" figures as mentors through Sunday School, youth ministry, and kids' clubs.

2. Affirm every gender-appropriate piece of imitation. Lit-

tle boys spontaneously walk, talk, and grow up following what Dad does. These are "high-fidelity" moments that need to be enjoyed and nurtured. The child needs to know that his partnership of imitation with Dad is received by the father and celebrated by the mother and significant others.

3. Affirm the quest for a "girl friend" from the earliest age you can imagine. Actually this is only the highest form of imitation of his perceptions of what a daddy is. To become a daddy, he knows he needs to choose a special woman. The good news Garth shared at the family dinner table was offered as a way of saying, "I want to grow up to be a husband and father. Today I found a girl who might someday be my wife." It was a very serious statement indeed for a eight-year-old boy.

THE TIGER ROARS

Del asked for personal conference time at a national youth conference where I was speaking. I thought he was one of the college-age counselors. At about six-foot-four and apparently very at ease with the counseling staff, I was not prepared for the truth. When Del showed up, I discovered he had recently turned seventeen, and was going into his senior year of high school the next month. "That's unbelievable!" I said, astounded. "You could get away with telling me you were twenty-one!"

Within two minutes, Del got right to the point of his conversation. He asked a question I am never quite prepared for: "How do I learn to love? I don't think I am a loving person. A lot of people offer friendship to me, but I keep them away."

Although I rarely anticipate this inner condition of loneliness, especially in sex-role packaged beautiful people, my response was ready from long and effective use: "How do you like being who you are?"

"I try not to think about that." He was uneasy with my question.

"Whatever for?" I probed.

"Because it would be indulging in pride—it would seem selfish."

"What if I told you that your problem with reaching out to others is that you cannot possibly treasure them if you refuse to respect and treasure yourself? It's hard for me to believe that you have any weakness in relating to other people, at one level, because you are so poised and seem to be at peace around everybody. You dress intentionally and tastefully, and you present yourself so positively in public. But on another level, I accept your cry of isolation. Around our kind of churches we have done a good job of knocking self-respect out of a lot of serious minded folks by our warnings about pride. But humility does not mean ignoring one's self or thinking badly of one's self. Instead, it means respecting ourselves so much that we work from that strong base to reach out to other precious people whose value we infer from our own self-respect."

I suggested to Del that Jesus got it right: Those who do not love themselves will be unable to love other people. "Love your neighbor as yourself" (Matt. 22:39) appears to be a command, but it is more likely an axiom or a general principle. It may even be a warning that you will be unable to love other people until you have a deep respect and thankfulness for being yourself. In a way much like we find in the Matthew 7:1 axiom, loving may have to cut both ways. Remember? "Do not judge, or you too will be judged."

"Come with me," I said to Del. I remembered seeing a large mirror in a guest lounge nearby. As we walked right up to our full bodied reflections, I said. "Look at those guys. What do you see?"

"A tall skinny kid with acne. He has skinny arms—no biceps at all."

"What else?"

"He slouches too much—needs to stand up straighter."

"Can I tell you what I see?"

He was bracing himself against my probable praise. I did not carry much weight with Del. He had met me only three days before, and then only as 1 of 2,000 people in a massive teaching session. Real clout comes from people with long-term contact. It is parents who make the greatest mark on the emerging sense of self-respect. Over two or three years as a mentor, I might provide important data for his weaving of meaning about himself, but not in an hour's conversation, most likely.

"I see a guy I thought was a college man, and one of the counselors here. Now that I've met him personally, I still find myself surprised that he could show so much dignity and quality at such an early age. But then, the same mistakes were made with me when I was seventeen. I think it came from some of the suffering I went through in high school. Look at that face of yours, marked with the hormonal signs of your new manhood, but also marked, perhaps, by some deep pain or humiliation. Something has ripened you very nicely."

My affirmation caught him off guard. It wasn't the undiluted flattery he had braced to reject. I could tell I had caught his attention at a very deep level.

"Give yourself permission to look in the mirror every morning and pray out loud with your eyes open. Thank God that He has created you. Form a prayer of thanksgiving something like this, 'I don't know why You did it or what You have in mind for me, but I thank You that You made me just like I am. I am grateful for the body You gave me, out of all of the millions of genetic possibilities I might have become. I accept my "image of God, male" gift too and ask You to help me to know what to do with its enormous energy and its need for lifelong love. I celebrate the good mind You gave me. And I thank You for getting my attention when I was young, so You could start early making me into the person You created me to become.' "

Del showed a remarkable ability to cope, at seventeen, with a fully adult body. Looking like he was in his twenties, with traces of acne still on both cheeks, he was the picture of the ideal emerging adult male. For reasons that are not entirely clear, the male hormone which saturates the baby boy from the ninth week of his conception continues to dictate profound realities in his body. These realities are witnessed in a number of significant areas of the male makeup.

Active energy. From first fetal movement to midlife, the male hormonal charge kicks males into higher activity levels than females. In *Bonding: Relationships in the Image of God,* I have described how energetic young boys are often penalized, especially in school and church classes. Young boys need action; to put them in crowded environments which demand long periods of passive silence violates everything that makes up a boy. In the early elementary years, it is common for teachers to request that parents get medication for their hyperactive sons, when in most cases their activity needs are well within the normal range. The number of children that should be handled by an adult boils down to this formula, never more critical than in working with young boys: one adult per the average age of the children. For example, eight children with an average age of four would require two adults to care for them. In a church nursery class, the department should be staffed by assigning one adult for every two or three children.

Bone structure. Unlike giant redwoods, humans grow to maturity and stop. While human growth is still shrouded in partial mystery, we do know that each bone in the human body carries a stop signal near the end of the bone section which signals maximum length permitted. We worry when a child breaks a leg, for example, lest the signal system be thrown off and uneven growth occur.

Males develop into slightly larger—that is, taller and thicker—skeletal models than corresponding females. Let me say it another way. Should the conception have carried exactly the same genetic material except for the gender selecting X or Y chromosome combinations, the XX female version would have been slightly smaller in stature and in bone formation than the XY male version. While part of the difference is in the genetic gender specifications, most of it is likely the result of the mother's male hormones pumped into fetal development and the long-term effects of the boy's own androgens. The volatile testosterone associated with the higher activity and restlessness levels in boys is especially at work.

Single-mindedness. I described in chapter 1 the androgen bath boys' brains get in the sixteenth to twenty-sixth week of fetal development. Looking at male behavior, it is not surprising to discover that the hormonal modification of the corpus colossum and of the left hemisphere predicts visible masculine behaviors. For one thing, the typical right-handed, right-eye-dominant male deals with almost everything in an efficient, single-minded rational way. He rarely talks about his feelings, emotions, beliefs, or aesthetic judgments. All men are well endowed with feelings, emotions, beliefs, and appreciation for beauty and truth. But those endowments in right-handed, right-eye-dominant men tend to be locked away in the hormonally sealed off but hungry right hemisphere from which no syntactical speech flows.

Another result of this single-minded male brain endowment, given the ability to block out their affective needs, is that men tend to become experts at keeping their minds on their business. They can easily focus on things they choose while ignoring distractions in their environment. In contrast to the typical female who processes everything through both affective and cognitive hemispheres (right and left), men are more likely to hunker down into tasks which hypnotically keep their analytical left hemispheres engaged.

When the typical right-side dominant man finds his feelings, emotions, beliefs, or aesthetic sensibilities rising, he may be reduced to tears, embarrassing himself because he seems to have lost control. You will see his feelings or hear them, often shamelessly, even noisily or angrily presented to you. His monosyllabic shouting, swearing, or obscene speech will tell you not only that he is outrageously angry and frustrated, but also that he "cannot put it into syntactical speech." And in his "kinder and gentler" moments when his capacity to love, to embrace truth, to make an irreversible commitment to God, or to feel the peak experience in a dramatic or musical presentation, is summoned, he is likely to be speechless. Even later, he may be unable to verbalize what he was feeling, although he was visibly in the grip of a profound yet unexplainable inner reality.

Knowing this great capacity of a man for giving himself to the grandest human vision, Jesus packaged His message in significant stories and parables. Men have little resistance to a story or to a generous and grand enactment of truth. So Jesus surrounded Himself with men of deep and profound commitment, and He still does. As men follow stories, their right hemisphere is activated and their values are carried along into revision. But when the Pharisees, exclusively men, would arrive to try to trick Jesus, they used left-brained, single-minded logical strategies, thus deliberately shutting down their beliefs and values, to keep themselves safely out of touch from Jesus' convicting teaching.

I referred to men's hungry right hemisphere with its feelings, images, creativity, and convictions. Their need for right brain stimulation no doubt accounts for the ways they listen to music, their fascination with stories which picture humorous events, and their vulnerability to those who pose moral or spiritual dilemmas in story or parable form. We will understand men better if we see their "single-mindedness" and their "speechless" responses as unique revelations of what men really are. When men want "affective" relief they turn to music, to story telling, and to jokes. If any movement or congregation falters in its ability to attract men to its ranks, check them out: they have failed to appeal to men's unique ways of processing beliefs and of making commitments.

Sexual pleasure. If you could see the Ciba medical drawing of genital development,[6] you would note that the pleasure center of the baby girl, the clitoris, reduces in relative size from the ninth week of fetal development until birth. At nine weeks, the pleasure center in the male and female are identical, are raised external to the body, and are remarkably prominent and visible. They are magnified again and both appear to be developing into an external penis in the twelfth week. Then between the twelfth week and birth the clitoris shrinks and is enfolded within the vaginal lips, but the head of the penile shaft continues to enlarge. Not only is the size of the pleasure center profoundly larger in the boy, it will magnify again at the onset of pubescence. This sensitive sexual pleasure organ is mounted on the end of the penile shaft which houses the urinary tract. This means that a male must deal with this high pleasure part of his anatomy at each urination event.

Cross-cultural examinations of the way males deal with the penis indicate the central place it plays in coming to manhood. The ancient Jew brought the penis under God's control through a faith-community-sponsored rite of circumcision. This tangible, physical reminder of God's covenant would be a very personal reminder to every Jewish boy of his special sexual accountability to God. The circumcised Jewish penis, should it turn up in a Gentile woman's bedroom or a house of prostitution, would witness against the male and accuse him of infidelity. Religious rites of circumcision continue in the Jewish and Muslim communities today. Many Muslim cultures postpone male circumcision until pubescence, accompanying it with elaborate rites of passage to honor the ripening sexuality of the young man. Menstruation, and childbirth, both rites of blood, are seen by some anthropologists as the young woman's rite of passage into adulthood. So most Stone Age and primitive rites for boys included bloody rituals involving scarring and pain as proofs of manhood status.

Among the Dani tribe in New Guinea a non-bloody penis ritual occurs. There, a phallic stick made of a hollow gourd is placed over the penis at the male rite of passage. This sudden change of status is postponed until the young man's external male genitalia become obviously mature. In this naked tribe the marks of maturity are easily visible with the budding breasts of the girls and the enlarging phallus and testicles of the male. The phallic stick may extend to several inches above the head of the male if he is of royal blood, or may be a modest waist height in a common-born male.

The phallic stick is the only "garment" the male will ever wear, except when he adds war regalia to his head and war paint to his body. The phallic stick is held in place by a spun tree root string which extends through the pointed end of the gourd and forms a loop around the scrotum, thus holding the penis cover in place like a giant artificial penis. This drawstring is then tied at the top end of the gourd: more tree-root cord is used to tie the upright penis stick around the waist for the shorter models and around the armpits for the regal versions. As an indicator of status the phallic stick displays a mighty extension to the penis, but as a public accountability symbol, it denotes that this penis is under tribal surveillance. The death penalty applies to any young man and his partner if he breaks protocol by prematurely using his penis with a woman without meeting public requirements for consummating sexual contact. No questions are asked. The death penalty has nothing whatever to do with issues of pregnancy or disease transmission. Cultures which institute a death penalty for premature or inappropriate sexual contact are addressing the "out of control" possibilities. They recognize that the pleasure center can dominate the life of a male, unless it is brought under community control and personal accountability for responsible use.

I first met Doug at a family camp when he was fifteen, then again three years later. He had survived his first week at a major state university, and a couple of shocking memories were very fresh. During his first twenty-four hours on campus, he had been solicited to join the campus gay organization. Then, late in the afternoon he was propositioned by an attractive, obviously seasoned senior woman, "How would you like to come to my apartment tonight and use your body?"

Doug's initiation invitations are an increasingly common temptation facing young men. It is clear that a culture which exploits this pleasure potential in its young males and which urges them to use their penises for their own immediate satisfaction, is robbing its young men of their dream of exclusive, lifelong marital intimacy and their likely ability to be faithful to one woman. It is also exposing them to a whole galaxy of potential sexual addictions which will dominate their lives. Quite apart from the painful individual tragedies such sexual pressure predicts, any society which tolerates sexual abuse and waste of its young is committing cultural suicide.

Fertility. The gift of "life," through the arrival of sexual ripening at pubescence, is easily the most treasured feature of sexual identity—for both healthy boys and girls. When they contemplate the possibility that they could "make a baby," they are looking at the power of their own creative fertility.

We are part of a culture which has trivialized the fertility of the young. We see more attention to fertility as the enemy than as the gift of life, that mystery of creative energy which enhances the value of being human. Our fear of the fertility of the young has us preoccupied about birth control devices and abortion. But among the young, there is a wonder and celebration that is waiting for our blessing, our empowering, and our encouragement to harness this powerful "image of God" energy for the achievement of their best dreams.

The arrival of menstruation is a marker for the young woman, and is commonly an event known among close family members. But the male's arrival at first ejaculation is often only inferred by parents or peers based on his sudden elevation in height or the appearance of facial and body hair.

Recalling the genital development discussion from chapter 1, you will remember the ovary/testicle part of the original anatomy. In the female these sources of fertility remain on location and shift into a horizontal position. At maturity the ovary will begin to release ripened seeds or ovum. Each ovary will ripen one seed about every fifty-six days, and the ovaries will alternate their ripening cycle so that in half that time—about twenty-eight days—first one, then the other, will release an egg.

When the ovary was transformed into a testicle and the pair were dropped into the vaginal-lip scrotum with the magical seal enclosing them and providing the sheath for the penis, the function of the ovary was changed. Instead of releasing the "seed of the original man," parallel to the woman's gift of life transmitted through the ovum from the "seed of the original woman," the testicle development actually activates a factory for producing sperm—the male seed. While the woman's ovaries are prepacked with a limited number of ovum—more than she could possibly use in the thirty-five to forty years of her fertility, sperm production in the male is virtually unlimited. There is no age limit, no menopause to shut down male fertility. The sperm are produced "from scratch," carrying no tracer back to "the original mother" as the ovum does. Beyond all of this, sperm are produced in absolutely incredible quantities. Consider the following minimums:

1. A healthy male will release about 300 million live sperm with every ejaculation. Extravagance is written everywhere in this aspect of male fertility, because only one of those sperm could possibly survive through meeting the ovum and joining to form a baby. The other hundreds of millions of sperm were just spares to guarantee delivery of at least one tremendously strong "wiggler" who beat all of the others to the available egg waiting in the fallopian tube.

2. The typical male is ripening that sperm harvest on an average of every forty-eight hours.

3. First ejaculation, at an average of thirteen years and three months, is typically followed by thirty-six months of increasing frequency of ejaculation which tends to set the adult appetite for pleasure and to reveal the healthy adult capacity for producing seminal material. Sperm and seminal fluids, all laced with various levels of the androgens, especially testosterone, are the lively activity fuel which drive males when their restlessness is compared to females. The sperm count, the amount of ejaculate produced, and the frequency of ejaculation vary widely among mature males.

This "tiger in the tank" is likely the least understood but most treasured gift of God to the healthy male. When I explained all of this nearly twenty years ago in a parent seminar at Hamburg Wesleyan Church in New York, I rounded out the biological material with a universal anecdote: "When Johnny reaches sexual maturity, it is Mother who most often finds traces of his masturbation or wet dreams, and Mother knows what ejaculate is when she sees it. So Mother says to Dad, 'You've got to talk to Johnny.' And Dad says he'll do it. But he doesn't. Do you know why Dad doesn't say anything to his son?" I asked.

I continued. "It is because dads are basically honest people, and they haven't yet figured out their own sexuality. So they stall. They simply can't bring themselves to lie to their sons. Silence is more honorable than pretending that they have the answers, when they still have serious questions themselves."

Suddenly I heard the clatter of two chairs to my right. I stopped and stared into the faces of two men who had collapsed backward as if in a reclining chair at home. Their feet, thrust forward, had sent folding chairs forward toward me, accordion-style. They had the look of men who had been ambushed by the police, caught red-handed in their crime. "Is there something wrong?" I questioned.

"I can't believe you know the scenario. We've just been through this at our house," one of the men volunteered. I wasn't surprised.

I conclude that the gift of fertility is God's first curriculum. It calls the young man to accept full responsibility for regulating his pleasure, treasuring his fertility for personal, community, and eternal purposes. When he makes a covenant of sexual responsibility, he will then harness his entire sexual energy in service of a lifelong, exclusive relationship with one woman whereby the two will become one. "-s49is not good for any human to be alone" is the primal wail of every healthy male.

TO BE IN LOVE
In the best of all possible worlds a young man sees, meets, and falls in love with a woman. Then he may find that she was orchestrating the whole thing all along because she had her own reasons for stalking him. Sexual energy and the search for love provokes males to a more complete use of the full brain than any other pursuit. In any social or cultural system a healthy man's dream of sexual pleasure unites with the high energy to be independent and responsible as an adult male. To these visions is added the distinct desire to be a father, that is, to extend his identity into time and eternity through the responsible management of his gift of fertility. Because of this great "desire," he takes initiatives, sometimes surprisingly assertive where he has been introverted in other contexts, and the "pair" appears. This consummation

leads to the matching of life vision with an exclusive life with one woman. With vocation and marriage intact, the circle is complete.

Most men have major chunks of unfinished business in hidden sexual secrets. Many of us have had no encouragement to believe that our sexuality was God's "image" witness to us, that our sexual energy was our highest potential and motor for the best and the most holy dreams we dared to dream. Human sexuality is shrouded in a veil of important privacy, but in that protected place it has often left us suffering in silence.

In this chapter I have offered a biological picture of developing male sexuality to connect the sex system to intrinsic male needs and motivations. And by comparing male and female development, I have wanted to offer a way for every man to face the woman of his dreams and sense that this baffling "otherness" is profoundly "bone of bone, flesh of flesh," the same stuff though radically different.

While there are many "under construction" areas in men's lives, the first and most persistently demanding arena where we have to keep working is in coming to honest terms with our sexual energy and appetites and our need for intimacy based on absolute mutual respect. The chapters which follow will never stray far from this sexual core of male identity and need.

 ## Do-It-Yourself Tips

Grab your boyhood photo album, or gear up the slides, home movies, or videos that will let you talk to the little boy you once were. Make this a private viewing:

1. Bless the little guy [use memories of actual school or family pictures if you can't get to your file of photo history] and tell him one secret you now know about sex that he would have benefitted from knowing. Grieve with him a little if he suffered because no one blessed him and gave him tools for thought in those tender and innocent years.

2. Carry these pictures in your mind and give yourself permission, on the edge of sleep, to carry on a dialogue with the little guy. In your imaginary conversations, call him by the name you loved to hear as a boy. You can heal most of your pain as a child if you grab a pillow and make gestures of protecting the young boy while telling him that you are here now and you know how to take care of him, that you are sorry he was afraid or abused before you knew how to take care of yourself better.

Read or try your memory on Psalm 23, knowing that "The Lord is my shepherd" is the same comforting word that you want to have extended back into your boyhood.

Contractor's Crew Notes

Give an advance assignment to every crew guy to bring a childhood picture from home to share in this session. You go first, describing yourself, and working through the "stems" below:

1. "I think I see myself today in this little fellow . . . [telling physical characteristics you can see]. Do you see anything I'm missing?"

2. "When I was this little guy, I was really glad to have been born a boy. I remember feeling. . . ."

3. "The thing about my sexuality that drove me to God and to wanting to answer to God was. . . ."

4. "The one thing I know now about sex that I hadn't a clue about then is that . . . and I wish someone had helped me to understand that."

Huddle up in your crew circle. Review the eyes and remember the stories you've shared today. Give the men a charge from the Apostle Paul: "This is the will of God—your sanctification, that you abstain from fornication." Let the prayer time be one of presenting all sexual energy to God for thorough sanctification and empowering.

CHAPTER FIVE

BONDING: WHO COULD LOVE ME AS I AM?

At least once a year at Asbury Seminary I teach a course called "Discipleship Development in the Home." Each semester, part of the curriculum of reading and reflecting examines things that have gone wrong with families. In one recent class, a team of three presenters were all single young adults. One surprised even herself by making a disclosure of childhood sexual abuse. Another had been profoundly damaged by a broken engagement. A third, coming from a single-parent urban home, had been traumatized in ways at which he only hinted. All expressed serious reservations about whether marriage and family life, inviting as they were in the abstract, could likely deliver the goods for a satisfying long-term prospect.

I sensed a cloud of empathetic grief and sadness hovering over the room of nearly fifty students, so in the closing moments, I said, "Is there a married person here who would like to say a word of hope to these folks?" I have a pretty high tolerance for ambiguity, and the bleakness of prospect we had experienced for more than forty minutes was a perspective worth contemplating. Still, I am an eternal optimist, so I cast my line upon the sea of faces. There were no volunteers, but I saw Chris Kiesling about ten feet from me with a grin and a glow that made my invitation a safe bet. I had the luxury of listening to Chris and Suzanne discussing possible wedding dates within minutes of our first meeting at a leadership conference in Amarillo some two years before. So I gambled:

"What good word can you give them, Chris? You and Suzanne have been married now for more than a year."

In an instant, his response began, and even though class was ready to end, his words were terse and piercing: "Everything about our marriage and wedding was a revisitation of my conversion."

The roomful of students was entranced by that single sentence, spoken softly in response to a professor's probe. Chris went on, "In marriage there is a completion of yourself. There is a making of a commitment to live completely under the scrutiny of another person. It is as if 'iron sharpens iron,' as Proverbs 27:17 says, yet the alteration of my own identity and self is happening in the midst of a gentle, warm relationship. What you can find in marriage that you can't find in being single is a relationship where you can risk being completely honest. You can be fully exposed and vulnerable and still find the intimacy of knowing you are in the arms of a person who loves and cares for you unconditionally. That's why Suzanne's love for me is a reminder of my conversion. Marriage and salvation both rest on unconditional love offered in exchange for complete honesty."

The bell rang. Everyone was stunned. The panel of discouraged presenters remained seated at the front of the room behind me. Chris' peers filed out in silence. I finally recovered enough to say something affirming. Then I asked Chris, "Where did that come from?"

"Well, as usual, there is a story behind it."

"Can we hear it tomorrow?"

"Sure."

"Remind me at the beginning of class, and we'll look into your heart at more of the implications about your marriage reminding you of your conversion."

I went ahead with the class agenda the next day. Chris, characteristic of him, did not remind me to let him finish his story. But near the end of the period, I caught a glimpse of

Chris and remembered. So I introduced him, inviting him to the front of the room. I led off:

"Yesterday, Chris blew us all away by revisiting his marriage to Suzanne and disclosing that its culmination was a revisitation of his conversion. I learned that there is a story behind the theology he opened up for us. I have no idea what it is, but here's Chris."

Chris began slowly, "One day when Suzanne and I were dating, she was baby-sitting for Steve and Thanne Moore's baby boy, Madison. The Moores were the directors of the Wesley Foundation at Texas Tech where we had met. Suzanne had been with Madison all day, and I went up late that day, eager to see Suzanne, but also wanting some time with Madison. I had not done much baby-sitting, so I looked forward to practicing my fathering skills. Suzanne had been having a lot of fun all afternoon with him. She wanted me to have a little experience with the baby. Suzanne handed Madison to me. Immediately he began to cry. I could not find a way to quiet him. Suzanne eventually took him back to his room. It was his bedtime, so she put him in his crib.

"In the brief time that elapsed a kind of rush of shame came over me. I realized that I had the potential of being a good father, but had never been put in a situation where I could try it. To be in a situation where I had that opportunity, and for the child to burst out with what seemed like a total rejection of me, released an avalanche of lifelong episodes of rejection. I felt like Madison's rejection of me was not based on anything I had done to him, but was simply his rejection of me as a person—because of who I was.

"I collapsed on the couch, and I began remembering and re-experiencing the many experiences of humiliation I had been through. I remembered a time in junior high school when I was asked to crown the cheerleader elected as Valentine's Day queen. It was expected that I would give her a big kiss on the lips with everyone applauding after I had placed the crown on her head. But, losing my nerve, or because my sense of boundaries checked me, I simply pecked her on the cheek. The beginning crescendo of applause for the queen turned into a violent *Boo* from my fellow classmates. I walked back to the bleachers surrounded by this wall of humiliating taunts. I remembered how ashamed I was and feeling like a failure at everything I tried.

"I remembered too feeling like I was a hopeless weakling in ninth grade. I was a tall kid, and the coaches yelled at me, humilating and degrading me because I was not able to lift weights well enough to satisfy them. All of this humiliation of my past began washing over me like a tidal wave. Overwhelmed, I lay there crying on the couch in the director's living room. Immobilized, I collapsed and shook with sobbing shame, remembering the many rejections I had experienced.

"Suzanne came in from the other room, sat down, and put my head in her lap and just let me cry. She simply held me. I relaxed completely. Slowly I realized that there was no reason in the world why I deserved that childhood rejection. I saw that everything ugly and vile that I had suffered was suddenly exposed to Suzanne. Yet she was saying, 'It's OK. I love you.' To me it was the most profound experience of pure grace I had ever experienced from another person. I began to understand what it is not to earn, not to feel like there was some performance I had to demonstrate, before I was worthy of love. Here was a complete relinquishment of everything I was to another person—in my ugliest moments of painful memory—accompanied by Suzanne's acceptance expressed simply and freely, 'It's OK. I love you!' "

Then Chris, turning to some of the students who had expressed serious questions about marriage and fears about leaving singleness, went on saying, "This is not the end of my story. Before I was reduced to emotional nakedness in front of Suzanne, there was only one other place that I was experiencing grace. That was in my time alone with the Lord. This led me to wrestle with the apparent contradiction between my need for companionship with Suzanne and my need for solitude and private devotion to God.

"I was then reading Mike Mason's classic *The Mystery of Marriage*.[1] He tells the story of his struggle between becoming a monk and getting married. The book opens as he is taking his new bride to visit the Trappist monastery where he had been accepted to become a monk. Mike Mason had worked with the contradiction in a way I was not having to do. In his tradition, he struggled between mutually exclusive choices—between the call to solitude and grace or the call of love and marriage. But he saw that the call to become a celibate monk and the call to marriage are essentially the same call. In both cases Mike saw that he would have to surrender everything. Both monastic orders and marriage are calls to give the self away.

"So, I saw that there was really no contradiction for me either. If I pitted my privacy and total devotion to God as a single male against love and marriage, I had not understood the integrity required of me to be totally devoted to God and single. To remain single as an act of freedom to fit my own scheme, even for devotion to God, would ultimately be an act of arrogance and privatism. I saw that whether I chose single-ness to perfectly practice my devotion to God or marriage, I would end up in the same place. I discovered that I would really find myself only when I gave myself away with no strings attached. The difference might be that the single person could find that surrender through solitude and through sweating drops of blood in a private Gethsemane. But the married person might expect to find it through shared companionship and walking through the marriage and family vows in a kind of corporate Gethsemane.

"What grace did for me through Suzanne after flunking the fathering test reminded me of the painful realities behind the Superman stories. A mediocre news reporter who often missed the big story and muffed details in embarrassing ways, who was weak, incompetent, and never destined to achieve greatness, also had a great secret. No one knew how he did it, but he could, in the face of major catastrophes, slip into a telephone booth, change clothes, and emerge with a red cape and superhuman powers.

"In my experience, somewhere down the line, I suspect that I will find freedom from my own feelings of weakness, incompetence, and inhibition. Chris Kiesling may actually perform incredible acts of servanthood and ministry. In my imagination I see my spirit taking off, soaring, and 'leaping over tall buildings in a single bound.' And in my dreams, I think that I will be able to look back and identify the 'phone booth' where I was reduced to nakedness, shedding the ordinary clothes that represent my weakness. My feelings of inferiority and humiliation evaporated there, and I was able to slip into special super clothes. I'm sure that when I turn to look at the 'phone booth,' its illuminated sign will simply read MARRIAGE."

IDEA BONDING

Chris gave us a picture-window view into one of the final closure events in his pursuit of marriage with Suzanne. His experience is enough to suggest some main lines in a theology of marriage. Chris was healed from damaging memories and devastation; this caused him to gain a new self-esteem. But we know that their relationship began long before that moment of vulnerability through humiliation. They must have spent their entire lives getting ready to be unconditionally "present" to each other.

Imagination. The vision of life fulfilled through an exclusive, lifelong intimacy is buried deep in the heart of every growing child. From infancy, given access to both a father and a mother, children infer the hope that somewhere, sometime there will be an "opposite" to love them, to hold them, to make life tolerable, and to share its ecstasies. I use the word *imagination* to describe future possibilities based on present realities. Chris and Suzanne must have had a "curriculum" of trust surrounding them from childhood. From the building blocks of early relationships they could "image" a future in which intimacy sealed a new unit. It could never fully prepare them for the vulnerability, or the unconditional accepting and acceptance that might be involved, but they were rehearsing, getting ready.

Relationship. In the ideal scenario, a young couple will each be in touch with their real sense of "need." There is a cosmic loneliness that hangs like a cloud of hope motivating the search for the "other." There is the time invested before a mirror asking the urgent question, *Will there be anyone who will love me for who I am? I can never make myself into a desirable person unless someone sees more in me than I see in myself.*

During our own long months of engagement, separated from Robbie by a thousand miles, I tuned my radio at 11 o'clock each night to WLW, eager to hear the theme music and poetry featured on the radio show, "Moon River," which I could sometimes pick up from Cincinnati. I bought the 78 rpm record of Mary Carolyn Davies' litany of love which I heard often on "Moon River." In answer to her question, "Why do I love you?" I could resonate with the incredibly plausible response, "I love you not only for what you are, but for what I am when I am with you." The reality of my own emotional bankruptcy engulfed me each time the lines reached the crescendo: "I love you because you are helping me to build of the lumber of my life not a tavern but a temple."

The sense of vulnerability and dependency are all but overwhelming in the solitude of the human condition. C.S. Lewis, in an amazing but little-noticed poem entitled "As the Ruin Falls,"[2] suggests that it is the awakening of profound love for another that reveals the past self-centeredness of all of life. It was all simply "flashy rhetoric about loving you," he confesses. "I never had a selfless thought since I was born." Trapped inside his own skin, it is love that has drawn him out until his heart is being fashioned into a "bridge" to reach his beloved and thus to embrace mature manhood. And now, even though "the bridge is breaking," he says, "The pains you give me are more precious than all other gains." Indeed, to become human and to have the dignity of loving and being loved is worth whatever risks of pain that might come. Healthy loving always focuses on the person, not on any of the rewards that might be stolen from another simply to satisfy an appetite.

Conversation. The original male was provoked to the first coherent human speech by the sight of the newly formed woman: "This is now bone of my bones and flesh of my flesh; she shall be called Ishah, for she was taken out of Ish" (Gen. 2:23, my translation). In a similar way, every man is called out of his silence by the attraction of a special woman. Young men, who rarely speak a complete sentence to their parents, can talk by the hour to magnetic women who call them to rise above their single-minded affectional silence to put their feelings into words. Some males write poetry only during their high romance period of life. Occasionally they will be inspired to set words to music. Strange and wonderful emotions arise, providing the energy that characterizes the dialogue of young men in love.

Touch. We nuzzle our babies, cuddle our toddlers, and wrestle with our young children. But when boys hit pubescence in this culture, they typically pull back, distancing themselves from parents and adults who would still like to hug them. We get to touch our teenage sons and grandsons in ritual moments; those hellos and goodbyes provide virtually the only moments during which a quick hug can occur. It is as if they are intentionally on a "fast," abstaining from the much-needed physical expression because of an intuition that sometime, somewhere, someone will come along who can satisfy the growing "skin hunger" that keeps them vulnerable as they launch into their search for love.

Intimacy. If marriage can be characterized by "knowing as we are known," then Chris and Suzanne were on the threshold of marriage, but could hardly have know it when Chris collapsed into his deep memories of humiliation. Suzanne was seeing Chris as he really was. He may be her Superman, but he will never be fantastic in the sense of being unreal. His strength will rise from the reality of this vulnerability and his revisitation of his memories of rejection and helplessness.

Paul Pearsall, in his book *Super Marital Sex: Loving for Life*, reminds us that super marriages are based on absolute transparency and disclosure. The intimacy we all need must be built from a foundation of honesty, not by masquerading our weaknesses or past misadventures. Pearsall, having studied one thousand couples with five-year follow-up in his Problems of Daily Living Clinic at Detroit's Sinai Hospital, concludes that intimacy must be built on complete honesty between the marital couple. Pearsall also currently serves as the director of professional education for the Kinsey Institute for Research in Sex, Gender, and Reproduction. He takes the position that our unmarried young people should not be having sexual intercourse, and that they are damaging their future marriages if they do.

"Sex is not like tennis," Pearsall writes. "Practice does not make perfect in sex, it only leads to more practice."[3] It turns out that "more practice" in sex is practice in promiscuity.

Pair bonding studies show that genital contact must be postponed until a couple has completed the curriculum of history giving, hammered out their values, and taken full responsibility for the lifelong needs and integrity of each other. If genital contact precedes these agendas in the twelve-step sequence, the bond will be profoundly weakened and is susceptible to marital failure. Pearsall is giving up-to-date professional and clinical evidence in support of the pair bonding sequence implications.

PREMATURE BONDING

It was a week of luxury for me. I had lots of free time at a week-long family camp where the schedule provided leadership other than my own. Early in the week, working through the lunch line, I was startled by seeing a young man I had not noticed before. As he turned facing me, virtually shoulder-to-shoulder, I saw his good face and at about fourteen his stunning new manhood was written all over him. Without any introduction at all, I simply blurted out, "I don't know whether anybody has ever told you or not, but you are dangerously good-looking. And if you don't give it all to Jesus, you're in big trouble!"

Evidently Brad already knew who I was—the camp grandfather and teacher of an adult seminar. At any rate, my comment triggered a sudden outpouring, "There's this girl who's been chasing me for two days and says she wants to date me," he whispered eagerly.

"See what I mean?" I laughed, and dismissed the exchange.

A day later Brad's mother approached me. I had seen her in all of my sessions, but had not seen her with Brad. "My mother was with Brad when you spoke to him in line yesterday," she reported casually.

I smiled, "That's wonderful. He's an amazingly good-looking young man."

"Well, you really made his day, and ours too," Brad's mother went on. "I really wish my husband could have been here this week, but he couldn't get off work. So I'm here with the children and my mother is along to help. Brad is our oldest. In fact, my mother has never forgiven my husband because I got pregnant with Brad on our high school senior trip. We were both out of good church families, and it crushed them all. We got married, and you now know the rest of the story about the fourteen-year-old boy that came from that misadventure."

The scenario of premature bonding often carries layers of pain, and in this case a very persistent layer of shame. But the chief pain of premature genital contact in a healthy bonding relationship is the "crisis" it brings as two people scramble to guarantee they will never have to say goodbye. They are ready to climb every mountain to protect the "forever bond" and take it into the public display.

"Take along a copy of my *Bonding: Relationship in the Image of God* and read it with your husband," I encouraged her. "You will see your story there—the Bill and Betty story—but your story has a delightfully happier ending than theirs. Congratulations on a super marriage and on a super son. I suspect all of the children are as wholesome as Brad."

Brad's parents were exclusively bonded. They survived pressures from disappointed parents, but the bond only was forged under hotter fire. His parents took full responsibility for their intimacy, and foreclosed their childhood and adolescence in favor of protecting the pregnancy and their own relationship. We rarely see stronger bonds than this, even though they didn't "make it to the church on time." If such couples could be studied systematically, we would likely see this "marriage" of pleasure and responsibility forming an indestructibly tough bond. Couples who abort pregnancies, or who are clever enough to avoid the pregnancy while stealing the pleasure, often live to yearn for integrity like that which welded Brad's parents into a super marriage.

DEALING WITH GHOSTS
I met Carl while lecturing at a university. He first left a message at my hotel. As I read and reread the note I examined Carl's name. Sure enough, his father and I serve on a national board of directors together. His dad had told me of giving my *Bonding* book to a son who was getting married.

Carl inquired whether I could save my Wednesday lunch hour to eat with him and his wife. I accepted the invitation and Carl and Gayle took me to lunch at the college grill. There he reported Gayle's continuing descent into hell as she replayed fantasy scenarios of Carl's late teen escapade of "living in" with an older woman. Carl summarized his painful story of sexual adventure in rebellion against his parents, and the trouble and agony that followed—all news to me! At the end of his rope, he told how he came in repentance to Jesus, enrolled in a Christian college, and eventually fell in love with Gayle.

Before proposing marriage to Gayle, Carl sought to clear the slate, so he gave her a detailed confession of his three lost years between leaving home and being reconciled to his parents and to his faith. Instead of letting go of the honest disclosure Carl had given her, Gayle seemed to be reviving it and breathing life into it more powerfully every day.

Carl sat there in the campus restaurant, in full view of his peers, his eyes flooding with uncontrolled tears. I watched as he mopped them up with napkins from the table dispenser. "You are married to a remarkable man," I told Gayle. "Diogenes can throw away his lantern. You have found an honest man. Most men would settle for a mediocre marriage rather than going to the root and hauling out the truth of their adolescent rebellion and sexual misadventures. But let me make a prediction," I said to Gayle. "You may be keeping Carl's old adultery alive when he has let it go. In fact, you may be making it more vivid than it ever was to him. And if you can't let it go, it is likely to boomerang on you. You are very likely to develop such resentment that you will plot to get even with Carl. You are going to be vulnerable to having an affair just to hurt Carl. But he has suffered so much for so long that he's less vulnerable to an affair than you will be.

"Let me offer you a strategy. Remember that whatever you are feeling is OK. But it is not OK to revive the ghost of Carl's past affair, a previous bond now long since buried and dead. I'm going to ask you to write your feelings—toward Carl, toward that three-year-live-in woman, and toward anyone else who may come to mind. You can name them and write as if you were telling them exactly what they have done to you and to your marriage. Send all of them to me and mark the outside of the envelope 'for your files only,' and I will never open it, but you will know that you said it all, once, on paper."

Gayle agreed to write out all of her grievances and to mail the document to me. Three months later, with nothing from Gayle, I wrote to the two of them.

Gayle wrote back immediately: "I'm sorry I did not begin the writing I agreed to do. Thank you for taking me seriously. Two other counselors had told me to forget it, but you said my feelings were important and should be dealt with. After Carl and I talked in the grill that day, it seemed like all of my hurt was gone. If it ever comes back I will write it out and send it to you. Our marriage is healed, I'm sure."

Because sexuality is at the center of our personalities, it is also the first curriculum of our moral responsibility. Everything about sexual feelings and behavior is colored with the ecstasy of the "ultimate good" or the tragic pain of the "ultimate evil." With sexual matters there is very little that falls within the middle ground between good and evil.

This mysterious gift at the core of human existence is the source, all at once, of: (1) personal identity; (2) pleasure; (3) reproduction; (4) the "two into one" glue of pair bonding. It is this "epoxy bond" by which two people are laminated into one heart, one energy, and one vision.

DEALING WITH CASUAL SEX

"I'm a little uneasy about opening this subject up for you guys who are single, but I need help. It may even be that my experience will mean something to all of you." Dan was taking the floor, at his request, in a lunch network support group meeting where the unwritten rule is that the first agenda goes to a member in need of solving an immediate problem.

"You know I was married about six months ago, but you don't know that I was sexually active with five other women during my university days. Further, my wife and I had intercourse for six months before we were married. Sometimes I think of those women when I'm having intercourse with my wife. I feel guilty about that. I know it is not right. But what is really bothering me now is that the buzz just isn't there when we have sex now. It always was before I was married and I hate to think that it's gone forever."

Dan took questions from his peers. Two students discussed parallel accounts of coping with similar post-marital adjustment. "Have you worked on what Dr. Joy calls retroactive healing?" one of the group asked.

"No. What do you mean?" queried Dan.

In response, I unpacked my discovery that the experience of God's sanctification means, among other things, bringing honesty and integrity to all of life here and now. I am no longer put off by that text in 1 Thessalonians 4:3: "For this is the will of God, even your sanctification, that you should abstain from fornication" (kjv). It is pretty clear both from the Apostle Paul and from human experience that sexual energy is either going to be thrown around in fornication or celebrated in sanctification.

Overcoming life's sexual baggage requires revisiting the painful past and asking God to transform prior experiences. It means letting the God of Creation and Lord of sexual differentiation and pleasure make it whole and holy in your memory.

"Here is what it might mean for you, Dan," I began. "How old were you when you first had genital contact?"

"Seventeen."

"OK. You are now ready to love Carla exclusively and passionately for the rest of your life. In your own imagination, do this: Whenever one of those old images appears, take Carla back to that event when you were seventeen. Cut away that old image of a woman who must surely be joined to some other man by now. At any rate, repudiate her as ever again a sexual partner for you. Now 'laser beam' in Carla's image—your lifelong exclusive lover. I call this 'laser beam sanctification surgery on your memory.' Imagine that you have only been sexual with Carla. If you do this persistently, it will have a wonderful effect. It will restore your monogamous vision, and it will laminate all of your affection to Carla.

"In addition, do this wild and marvelous thing; imagine that, miracle of miracles, you were married to Carla before you had the contact at seventeen. The cultural taboos have been suspended—in this sanctified imagination—and from your first sexual union there has always been Carla—the other side of yourself. The surgery works all the way back to childhood, because imagination transcends legal marriage age and goes for what is true, right, holy, pure—and timely!"

Dan and Carla indulged in the luxury of eating the frosting off the cake before the meal was served. And where couples are "successful" in long-term sexual intimacy before marriage, they tend to forge an addiction to the "adrenaline high" that accompanies stolen escapades. When this happens, it seems to replace the healthy "endorphin high" that comes from intimacy that is celebrated and sanctioned by the community. Adrenaline high addiction, after marriage, needs to re-create the "illegal" and "secret" romance to be satisfied, and affairs are spawned in search of the addictive "high."

Dan and Carla took the pleasure, hit an adrenaline high, and "bonded" to destructive and addictive brain chemicals. They were hooked, addicted to forbidden pleasure without unconditional responsibility for each other and the new "persona" of their sexual relationship.

His support network recalled that Dan and Carla had hit a rocky spot late in their courtship when Dan had complained that he wasn't sure he was ready for marriage. His support group had interrogated him through the breaking of his engagement and helped him to see that he was running away from responsibility, making Carla only another statistic in his search for pleasure without responsibility. Dan's healing will be a process, but the prognosis is good when he yearns to bring fidelity and pleasure together in his marriage.

DAMAGED BONDING

In wrapping up this chapter I will identify in brief scenarios some of the booby traps which damage men. If men's secrets are ever revealed, the majority of them will include painful and deforming experiences which parallel or supplement these:

Instrumental sex. Males seem to be more vulnerable to separating sex from relationships than are females. As you reflect on the reasons I offered for this in chapters 1 and 4, let these stories help you better understand the broken bonds in your own world of acquaintances. Many couples, and men especially, are totally baffled about how they broke their marriages.

Ron, four years into marriage, is still unable to resist occasional visits to massage parlors where explicit sexual services are offered and adult bookstores where repugnant homosexual acts are done to him. I asked Ron to write up a complete history of anything remotely related to his present sexual misadventures which threaten to destroy his marriage. A likely root event showed up at age nine. Ron's older brother permitted Ron to hang out with him and his friends. One day the older boys, in their early teens, were excited because one of them had arranged for his girlfriend to visit while the boys were on the premises. The guys carefully rigged a "privacy corner" for the couple, but tiny peep holes were cut in the blanket that surrounded the corner of the basement. The older boy successfully talked his girlfriend into the spot and into removing her clothes for him. The row of onlookers were perched on the other side of the blanket. One of them, at the first sign of forbidden flesh, giggled. The girl abruptly jumped back into her clothes and ran out of the house. The event was regarded as hilarious by the whole gang.

"What connection do you see between that show, and your fascination with pornography and sexual encounters with strangers?" I asked Ron. His addiction to forbidden and "instrumental" sexual flesh was clear.

"Well, we were using her and didn't give any thought to what humiliation she might have felt. We did it for kicks."

"Exactly. And you are still doing it for kicks," I noted.

If Ron is to find healing he will have to take intentional steps to bring sexual pleasure exclusively into the intimacy of marriage. He is making a bold first step by telling the truth about his sexual past among trusted long-term friends. I serve as host, but he brings his support system with him. We are establishing reward and affirmation for Ron in exchange for his bold adventures toward truth and integrity. We will soon bring his wife in for a guest session with the network, as he reveals to her his intentional search for healing and for consummating an intimate marriage.

Masturbation devastation. During my early years of teaching, Mel walked in for an informal appointment. "I am a senior," he began. "I graduate in two months. I transferred here from another seminary and you don't know me. I've never had a class with you, but I've watched you. I think I can trust you. If I don't get one thing under control, I'm not going to be able to make it in ministry. And since I don't expect to ever see you after I leave here, I'm willing to tell you about it."

"Of course, you can talk," I said. "But I need to warn you that when people suffer together they may be stuck with each other for the rest of their lives. You may not be able to simply walk away from me if I have listened to you and bled with you."

Mel unfolded a story of persistent masturbation. No, his wife knew nothing about it, and she wouldn't be able to deal with the truth if he told her. Yes, the frequency was daily, sometimes more often. It happened whenever he was alone after his wife left for work or if he went back to the apartment for lunch.

I had my class notes from Boyd McCandless' lectures on the "male and female sex systems" from my study at Indiana University on adolescent development. He had used the term, "hydraulic system" in describing the powerful sexual appetite—not a drive!—that most males develop. But I had not tracked down his documentation. So I bought time with Mel and promised to get him some information to help him deal with his appetite turned compulsion. The summary of what I told Mel is found in the section *The Sex Systems* in a chapter called "Adolescence: Is There Life After Puberty?" in my *Bonding: Relationships in the Image of God.*[4] I assured Mel that he needed to break out of the habituated pattern, and immediately we needed to lift his sagging spirits. At that time I did not realize that a mild depression associated with his "wife at work, husband in school" syndrome often expresses itself in shame-driven secret masturbation.

"She'll have to know at some point," I said, "that you are defrauding her. All of your sexual energy belongs to her. But I'll help you get ready for that," I assured Mel. Self-hatred and low self-esteem are terrible tyrants. The cycles of compulsive behavior are all driven by motors of deeper and darker self-contempt. I took Mel into one of the very first campus groups I ever met with to widen his network of support as he struggled with devastated self-respect.

To the rescue. Since men are "fixers," and problem-solvers, always ready to help their women, a strange mixture of pity, affection, and sexual intimacy occasionally shows up. A pastor may indulge in pity while listening to a woman describe her terrible marriage, recent divorce, and lifelong yearning for someone to love her. He may find chords inside singing out, "Save her. Be the best lover she ever had. She deserves you."

I caution both men and women in ministry to avoid the pity trap. "There is one Savior, and that's enough," I teach. "Don't imagine that you can solve everybody's problem or be everything they need. But you can be the facilitator. You can put them in touch with resources in heaven and on earth. Just don't try to be a savior." I am equally adamant in squashing the heresy that pastors are "married" to the church. I often say, "The church has one husband: Jesus. That's enough. We can't have bigamy scandalizing the church. Be the husband of one wife, or the wife of one husband, and Jesus will affirm you for it, but don't go flirting with His bride."

I was moving quickly past the seminary bookstore one morning. The printer was running for me fifty feet down the corridor, so I stopped to check my mail.

"Dr. Joy!" a student hailed me. I turned around to exchange greetings, only to be stopped a second time. "Are you Dr. Joy?"

"I don't know you, though," I responded, walking toward a distinguished looking customer emerging from the bookstore.

"I'm Bill Miller. I practice law in Florence, Kentucky. I was in the area, so I stopped to buy some of your books. I'm glad to meet you."

Attorney Miller took six copies of *Re-Bonding: Preventing and Restoring Damaged Relationships*[5] from the shopping bag and asked, "Would you mind autographing these? If you had written this book three years earlier I think I could have saved my marriage. I was unfaithful to my wife, and I thought I was promiscuous. But when I read *Re-Bonding,* I was amazed to see that I was an adulterer and that I really could be cured.

"Now I give a copy of *Re-Bonding* to anybody who asks me to help them get a divorce. I've given away quite a pile of books to people, and it is cutting back on the number of divorce cases I work on."

Dan, whose story I tell in *Bonding,* found himself torn between his wife and a second woman. Eventually, his wife ended the marriage, unable to continue to share her husband with series of other women. It was Dan who shocked me into the reality that promiscuity (what the *King James Version* calls "fornication") and double-bonding (what the KJV calls "adultery") are very different disorders.

Both Bill and Dan were "tournament males" when I met them. It is likely Dan continues in his pattern of rescue and sexual loving. These competitive males, rarely vulnerable or able to tell the truth about their own needs, see themselves as competing for intimacy. If they provide well they deserve intimacy. If a woman seems relatively secure and able to care for herself, the tournament male will often be unfaithful. His first line of justification to his wife, upon being found out, tends to be, "But you didn't need me, and she did."

When Bill Miller described his adultery I detected a complicating symptom, so I picked up a copy of *Bonding* and read the definition of "tournament species" in the animal kingdom. They are easily identified by their crowns, colored feathers, or their combative antlers and horns. "You don't have the plumage or the rack of the wild kingdom, but you have money, prestige, and power. You are accustomed to ruling wherever you roam. The whole industrial world bows down before you. And if you want to be generous with a secretary whose husband has abandoned her, you have a right to do that. If she is lonely, you have the right to comfort her. You call the shots." He grimmaced at the truth of my accusation.

A few weeks later Bill called. "I have good news. My former wife has agreed to come with me if I can get an appointment." Seated in my office with her, Bill pulled a copy of *Bonding* from my shelf and read to his former wife his own sexual "obituary" from the "tournament species" section. In those animal and bird species, males gather harems—as many females as they can win and support—and compete against other males by using status, courtship rituals, and sheer power to gather their cluster. In humans, both males and females, that impulse occasionally surfaces and nourishes the idea that they deserve all of the partners they can win— and they want to keep them all. Then Bill closed the book and said, "I want to be through with that part of my life."

In the next chapter we will look in detail at the tournament male—"Competing: Scoring and Other Rewards." These "winners" enjoy a highly visible profile in our culture. In this chapter I have sought to establish the base for lifelong exclusive bonding. With that vision in place, we must have further agendas for crews of "men under construction" as they find ways to make peace with their past and with their enormous sexual energy.

Do-It-Yourself Tips

Check your own "image potential" in the Creation picture of "Adam" split into female and male parts in Genesis 2. Here "Adam" is now "Ish" the male and "Ishah" the female. You can review—don't trust your Sunday School story memory on this one—in Genesis 5 of the *New International Version* where "God blessed them and called them 'Adam.'" (Check the footnote where "man" turns out to be "adam.") And in Genesis 2:23 "Woman" and "Man" are revealed in the center column of the *New American Standard Version* to be those very different words: *Ish* and *Ishah*.

Now, browse through Song of Songs (or Song of Solomon as most of us have known it). Locate a translation such as the NASB which provides tips on the bride's speeches and the groom's speeches. Look at the sexual intimacy language and try to crack the picture symbols for the intimacy gestures they represent. This song of exclusive sexual loving celebrates the importance of lifelong monogamous sexual intimacy. Revisit your own journey of intimacy and finetune it with the Genesis and Song of Songs reminders.

Contractor's Crew Notes

As facilitator of the session, come armed with the Genesis and Song of Songs excerpts suggested in "Do-It-Yourself Tips." Let them set the stage for some easily remembered history:

1. "As I recall the best of my own efforts at pursuing

exclusive love, I felt most successful, most truly masculine and loving when. . . ."

2. "If I could do one thing differently in my present marriage or serious relationship, it would be. . . ."

Huddle up for a crew covenant of eyes and affirmation sealed with supportive prayer that focuses on specific shared hopes and yearning for forgiveness and healing.

CHAPTER SIX

COMPETING: SCORING AND OTHER REWARDS

When Magic Johnson's sexual "scoring" from his earliest days of basketball success was finally halted by the HIV virus, the unwritten law of the athletic event surfaced in high profile. Wilt Chamberlain had recently bragged about his 20,000 sexual conquests while on the high road of basketball success.[1]

Everybody likely notices it, but some men go crazy when a woman shows up in their environment. I've been stunned and offended by the drawn knife in the quick hand of one of my backpackers when a team of bikers that included women rode into our campground. He was asserting his "rights" to impress the women and actually drew blood from an imagined competitor.

The phenomenon even shows up in the seminary gym when women file into the empty bleachers to cheer an intramural game. A few of the guys change personalities.

Anyone can speculate about why some males slip into a display mode when there are women present. But anthropologist Melvin Konner offers some provocative speculations in a chapter entitled "Lust," from *The Tangled Wing: Biological Constraints on the Human Spirit.* The book is both sensitive and shocking. In it he describes the behavior of tournament species animals and birds. Konner reports, for example, that

4 percent of the competitive bulls in a herd of elephant seals will impregnate more than 85 percent of the females. Breeding rights are won by persistent violence against other males. Indeed, among tournament species across the animal and bird kingdoms there are an amazing and illuminating series of common characteristics. Consistently in these male-dominated species:

1. Males are fiercely competitive for breeding rights, with a flamboyant display of visible "sex markings" such as highly ornamental color, tufts of feathers, or antlers used in fighting and defending turf.
2. Males are polygynous. They have an open number of females in each mating season, depending on successful competition and on the availability of an adequate food supply to support the harem.
3. Males form a hierarchical structure, with the most powerful and successful males both controlling their harems of females and competing for herd status.
4. Males have a low investment in the care of the young, and in some species seem intent on destroying the newborns.[2]

In *Bonding: Relationships in the Image of God,* I go on to discuss the amazing characteristics of the nontournament species. Konner's descriptions are at least a parable to instruct us about patterns in human pair behavior. The "perfectly bonding" species of animals and birds are exclusively monogamous, often mating for life and surviving alone after the loss of the original partner. They are nonhierarchical in their pair behavior and do not run in hierarchically organized herds. They move toward mating through a long and elaborate pair bonding ritual, with nest building completed before breeding. Then they share the care of the young, some males even having a capability to feed which matches the mother's natural feeding resources.

MALE DOMINANCE

When human males control and abuse their women and children it is inevitable that we would look for some way of explaining such behavior. The Marquis de Sade is said to have figured it out this way: "Since human males are larger and more powerful than females, it therefore is clear that they should control their women." We have used his name to coin a word describing violent assaulting behavior by a powerful person upon a weaker person: sadism.

George Gilder, in his book *Men and Marriage*, describes another equally secular theory. Men need women to care for them, bear their young, and feed them. So men enter into sexual contracts with women by which they gather the food (or money) in exchange for the protective home, hearth, and sexual privileges the women can furnish.

The Judeo-Christian doctrine of Creation and Fall offers yet another theory. Man and woman were formed out of the original Adam. They were granted dominion as co-regents and joint-heirs of the promise. But two differing kinds of moral failure separated them: the woman was deceived by the serpent, and the man rebelled knowingly against the directions of the Creator. So two kinds of consequences fell upon them.

The woman was predicted to have complicated problems in all of her primary relationships. She would be the victim of increased complications and pain in childbirth. She would "desire" her husband, literally would turn from desiring or worshiping God and would turn her man into her god. He would retaliate by unilaterally controlling her—"He will rule over you" (Gen. 3:16).

The man was predicted to become absorbed in his work. His frustration would mount as he tried in vain to subdue the material universe. The silence about his awareness of need for significant relationships is interesting. Lastly, he takes away his wife's co-regal name—*Ishah*—and replaces it with a name for functional chattel, "Eve—the baby maker." The woman quickly returns the deformed "compliment." From then until today, Hebrew and Israeli women refer to their husbands as *Baal*, my idol, my "lord." So the curse is alive and well in all cultures where women love too much, depend too much, idolize too much, and men, from that high and godlike position, exploit their women by "ruling over them" in chain-of-command marriages and harems.

Within the space of three chapters in Genesis the idyllic vision of "two becoming one" is shattered. Emerging is a male who will dominate Eve and her sisters, indeed a harem of women, across millennia. Jesus counters this vision with His exclusive pair bonding summons to one man and one woman to be "joined together, let no one separate" (Matt. 19:6, my translation).[3]

CONTROLLED BY INSECURITY?

Why would any man have his eye on a harem of women? Ben shared with his support group how at thirteen he was stunned by his best friend. Ben already had a vision of one exclusive, lifelong lover whom he would find and marry. But a friend confided to him one day, "I can't imagine living my whole life and having sex with just one girl." Ben was speechless, unable to comprehend how any guy his age could think that way. Ben's young friend may have been a witness to his parents' infidelity, and if his father was openly pursuing other women, the boy was a good learner. Or was he simply a "fallen male" with this central tendency to regard women as objects to be used by men?

Indeed, when a young man grows up seeing girls as "objects" for his satisfaction, visually or genitally, the universal effects of original sin are in motion as "competition, greed, and acquisition, even hoarding." A collection of "trophy" women as "sexual conquests" nicely fulfills that original sin desire. In our culture, as in many worldwide cultures, the promiscuous, "on the make" competitive male is viewed as "normal," even attractive in his demeanor.

For example, a number of years ago, Phyllis George did a halftime interview with Dallas Cowboy quarterback Roger Staubach and asked him point blank, "How does it feel when you compare yourself with Joe Namath who is so sexually active and has a different woman on his arm every time we see him?"

Roger, as cool on camera as in the pocket of Tom Landry's

"shotgun" offense, reported, "Well, I'm sure I'm as sexually active as Joe. The difference is that all of mine is with one woman."

When my "Discipleship Development in the Home" class discussed Magic Johnson's announcement that he was HIV positive, I was pained to find among the nearly 100 written comments this one from a vibrant young seminarian who had had a brief semi-pro hockey career:

> I was not surprised to learn that Magic Johnson had been promiscuous with a lot of "groupies" that hung on to him. Even though I was on a fairly obscure farm team as a semi-pro hockey player, there was a rule that I was expected to follow: If you score on the ice, you must immediately score in bed. With the beautiful female fans that hung around, it was easy to find flesh for scoring.

Kings David and Solomon faced similar temptations. Their kingly conquests obligated them to take new harems of women to match their international reputations. Everything between Genesis 3 and Jesus illustrates the "fallen male and female" syndrome of deformed relationships. And when success comes to almost any man today, he is increasingly vulnerable to the idea that he "deserves" to have as many women as he can manage without messing up his career and his marriage. Well, at least his career.

Here is a key factor to consider. Is male competition for female attention driven by low self-esteem and insecurity? Does each new fast-lane achievement only require a "higher high" to satisfy the next time around? How else do you account for the tragic path of sexual misconduct by so many religious and political leaders? Are such men hollow, or simply filled with worries that drive them to a competitive mating style?

Low self-esteem may, indeed, masquerade itself as high self-esteem. Arrogance does characterize many of these competitive, polygynous, tournament men. They leave the child care and child rearing to the wife. "Women's work," they call it. Control of income and wealth is exclusively their domain, and often it is collected and banked secretly, or just as secretly squandered. Since low self-esteem is a universal human trait, every male is vulnerable to buying into the tournament model of sexual animal.

The payoff, however, more often than not, is devastating to tournament men who brag, "I did it my way." They tend to devastate the more monogamously programmed women, but in any culture which respects the value of women, they will find themselves having not only the devil to pay, but also their women and children.

BENEVOLENT DICTATOR?

When "on the make," the tournament male is able to move through all of the right steps in forming a courtship or pair-bond. He even makes the appropriate exclusive promises and follows through by making every effort to keep his multiple mistresses from having contact with each other. I recall a famous Dallas millionaire who managed to rear two families only a few miles apart. Only his will identified the second family as his own.

The tournament male is often Don Juan to the rescue for a woman in trouble. He will literally fight off her other suitors. Indeed, he loves to win his women through combat of sword or wits. Today's male most often does this through a show of money and power. The so-called marks of mid-life crisis in males—following teenage fads and displaying hot automobiles and fast-lane lifestyle—are most often signals of a reawakening tournament instinct.

Since the secret life of the competitive-tournament male is intentionally deceptive—in order to keep his sexual options open—the tournament husband tends to accelerate his high-control patterns. When he is pursuing or actually controlling and supporting more than one woman he is likely to seem happier, have higher energy, and be more sexual with his wife than when he is stagnant and not in a "winning streak." In contrast, a more monogamously oriented male will cease being sexual with his spouse when he is caught up in the emotional pursuit of an affair. In the monogamous male's adultery, he is at least "faithful" to his preferred lover.

The competitive-tournament male tends to supplement his amorous courting behavior with threats and violence to make it clear who is going to "rule the roost." Complicate his stress with alcohol or drug consumption, and it is anybody's guess where his need to control may take him or where his violence may strike.

FALLEN DESTINY?

It is easier to document the formation of the "macho" male than the more prevelant "tournament" male. Chapters 7 and 8 describe how damaged teenagers become self-protecting and fragile macho adults. But the "tournament" deformity seems deeper and nearly universal among human males. Melvin Konner's and George Gilder's theories may be universalized. They can "describe" the way things are, but the doctrines of Creation and Fall offer a very plausible explanation for how sin has deformed us all.

In his chapter on "Lust," Melvin Konner reports that 85 percent of animal and bird species are either nonbonding or polygynous tournament species dominated by larger and clearly marked males. He goes on, almost without noticing the parallel, to describe human male sexual behavior. The same percentage of human males tend, at some time or another, to experiment with trying to attract and hold multiple females. In many human cultures today, and in most human cultures across time, males have traditionally supported harems of women, often legally as in the Muslim and African cultures today.

George Gilder argues that the male determines to find a safe place to produce offspring and to keep his options open. His argument sees the male as relatively weak, highly insecure, and dependent on a resourceful and faithful female.

But the Scriptures describe the Eden sin as fracturing the bond, trust, and mutual respect that existed between the male and female *(Ish* and *Ishah)* who together form the image of God. The sin which "smashed the Adam," emotionally and spiritually, ushered them into a nuclear winter of broken relationships. While the woman was renamed "Baby-maker Eve" to denote her indentured function, the arrogant Adam, taking the racial name for himself alone, regards the whole creation as his property. He will name and control the whole thing—including the renaming of the woman.

The curse and consequences of Genesis 3 make it clear that males think about relationships differently than females. He is preoccupied with things. He will work, sweat, produce, putter, and be frustrated by his tools and his playthings, but relationships rarely seem to enter his picture, except to analyze them and reduce them to their "function." Hence, Eve—Baby-maker! Polygyny is implicit in this refocusing of woman's role. She is no longer lover and peer, but an object. And if her function determines her value, then woe is the woman if she is barren.

There is hope for healing from the tragic effects of the Fall. As with other effects—the complications and pain of childbirth, for example—it will take intentional confrontation to make a difference. Doing what comes naturally will consistently tend toward male dominance, even violence. Transformation will come only by intentional choice, by open repentance and apology, and by daily consistent practice of respect for women. This will cultivate the exclusive bond and bring the spouse back to her place as joint heir of God's grace and co-regent in the creative management of the household and of Planet Earth. All of this is wonderfully predicted by Joel and Peter, both of whom present this communication as the word of the Lord, "In the last days, God says, I will pour out My Spirit on all people. Your sons and daughters will prophesy" (Joel 2:28; Acts 2:17).

MARITAL RISK

Combining the nearly universal deformity of the competitive-tournament male with the damaged macho variety we will look at in chapters 7 and 8, it is clear for women that entering into a relationship with any man is a considerable risk. It is reasonable, therefore, to end this chapter with a list of cautions. They might be considered as bottom line truth-in-advertising statements. I offer them more as appeals to invite all men to remain "under reconstruction," to finish our business. And if our wives and our male friends will help us to articulate the truth, the damaging demons will be largely cast out. Together, we can surely be the instruments of each other's confession, repentance, and transformation.

1. Beware extravagant displays of power. The guy with the hot car who prowls the parking lots at high schools is exhibiting tournament muscle. The glamorous adult male who "displays" through extravagant clothing and the parading of playthings such as vehicles and high-tech sound systems is likely dangerous. These tournament males like to be seen in "full regalia." They hide behind closed doors when they are "unpresentable" for any reason. Remember this image: The tournament pheasant cock with extravagant display of brightly colored feathers, compared to the drab and plainly-dressed female, is out to collect a harem.

2. Beware the rescuer. The tenderest of the tournament males are likely to "display" by their caregiving. They are at their best when they can "fix" something for a woman. This may be an emotional hurt or a flat tire. Their worth seems linked to their ability to rescue and to "deliver." One version of the rescue is purely financial. Are you broke? Women, beware. He will bail you out. Are you poor? He will bring gifts to your children. The woman is forbidden to reciprocate; if there is any giving to be done, he will be the giver—except for sexual favors. And in these favors he sees himself most often as "providing her the real love she never has had." Thrown off balance by his gifts and financial extravagance in her behalf, she feels she must compensate and sees the sexual favors as her "payoff" of the debt she is accumulating in meals, gifts, rent and car payments, and other of his inappropriate extravagances.

3. Beware the "spiritual leader." Do a talk-show interview with women at Christian colleges. What do they want in a man? "A spiritual leader. I want him to be the head of the house." These distorted images nowhere occur in the doctrine of Creation or in Jesus' way of salvation and grace. Spiritual "idolatry," remember, is a result of the Fall. "Baal" is not a name for husbands denoting their spiritual vitality, but denoting the woman's inappropriate dependency and spiritual bankruptcy. A healthy man will be spiritually alive and growing, but in a Christian relationship, husband and wife are spiritually responsible to God and to look out for each other's moral and spiritual good. "Let them have dominion" and "Head and body" as "one flesh," as Christ and the church are one, are images of mutual submission and mutual empowerment through synchronized spiritual connectedness.

So a morally sensitive, monogamous male times his giving impulses to the growing seriousness of a relationship. His generosity may be enormous, but it will be released with discretion to avoid the impression that he is buying favors. Men often seem to realize that the bail-out strategy is a weak foundation for relationships. Men who marry after bailing out a woman often cannot discriminate between acts of charity and those of love. Those who fail to break free will begin a pattern of rescuing other women for most of their adult lives. If the women they love ever become strong, stable, and competent, these men will search out another woman in need. Their parting cry to a previous wife or lover echoes, "She needs me more than you do." He loves to be needed. He's a rescuer.

In this chapter I have described a central vulnerability in many men. The very thing that makes so many of us attractive to women is our competitive and tournament behavior. It is our seeming glory and certain downfall. We are lonely and scared. We need help from others to move on.

Do-It-Yourself Tips

Click off this test as you do your "mirror review" of your own history of ideas about relationships with women:

1. At twelve, did I have the idea that someday I would find

the "right woman" and marry her for a lifetime?

2. Did I go through a "series" of girlfriends thinking I should be able to "keep them all," or was I always ready to let one go before turning toward another?

3. Am I primarily "monogamous" in my spontaneous attraction, or am I primarily "tournament"? [If you conclude you are programmed in "tournament" tastes, can you ask God now to give you a heart for one woman, just as you are ready to abandon your many idols and turn toward one God?]

Contractor's Crew Notes

Are you ready now to open the door for some history giving that tracks with this chapter? Have your group discuss the following:

1. "I've seen 'tournament males' in action. In high school I knew this guy who. . . ."

2. "When I look in the mirror, I wonder how vulnerable I am to the 'tournament pattern'? Let me tell you how reading this affected me. . . ."

Bring Matthew 19:1-2 to the crew before you huddle to pray. Note that Jesus called for monogamy: one man, one woman, protected from interference from anybody! He was speaking this into the ears of polygamous Jewish men—each licensed to possess up to six wives simultaneously. They wanted to liberalize divorce laws to increase the number of women they could accumulate and use in a lifetime. Jesus said that divorce had been permitted "because of the hardness of your hearts!" Now, huddle and let your eyes review the stories you have shared. But put your hearts into God's crucible to be made tender and kept profoundly monogamous.

CHAPTER SEVEN

SURVIVING: TOUGHNESS THAT PROTECTS

The university auditorium was packed, more than 2,000 students attending a required convocation. I was making a point that promiscuous people are hurting people, though outwardly they are often the campus models of manner and style.

"Do you want to know what these young men look like?" I asked after setting the agenda for offering hope to the sexually damaged young adults on campus. "Do not imagine that they are aggressive and dangerous. On the inside they are hollow men. The mildly macho look is a thin facade by which they try to convince themselves that they are tough, independent, and in need of nothing. But there are so many of them that the image of the macho man has become the poster hero of late twentieth-century America."

With more than 2,000 students wall to wall, I was planted in the middle of one side of a wide auditorium. Gorgeous young adults were stretched a full 180 degrees from my left to right side. "Right now," I said, "if these hurting guys are in this auditorium, they want you to believe that they don't need anything, that they have it all together. To make this point they will pretend to be indifferent to everything. The most boring thing that could happen would be a university-sponsored, required-attendance convocation on sexual integrity and recovery.

"These deeply wounded young men will spread this morning's sports page across the lap and defy the speaker to get through to them. Don't take them seriously about this cool posturing. They give themselves away in their masks of humor, small talk, mild obscenities, and unwillingness to sustain eye contact. And if they are here today, they will be sitting on some distant perimeter wearing sunglasses, cocked back scanning the sports page of this morning's paper. These are all attempts to disguise their feelings of emptiness, shame, and inferiority." My statements were only conjectures; I had seen no newspapers or sunglasses in the auditorium.

Rodney made an appointment through a sign-up sheet in the dean of students' office after hearing my convocation address. My appointment roster was full that day. I had offered a path back to wholeness. "Is There Life After Promiscuity?" was the title of my morning address.

"How did you know me?" Rodney began our session.

"What do you mean?" I was baffled, and the convocation was now several hours past.

"When you described me, I folded my newspaper, tilted my chair down from its hindlegs, took off my sunglasses, and looked around me. Three of my friends were still buried in their sports pages. I thought, *Thank God! At least I heard this guy.* My buddies were still trying to look cool behind their newspapers. How did you know me?"

"The description found you because your name is 'Millions.' I've worked with a lot of guys who are tough on the outside, but they are wrecked and fragile on the inside, and they know it. When they start telling the truth, they are on their way to complete healing."

"Can you tell me how to get out of the rotten emptiness you describe? See, at age fifteen things were terrible at home, so I left in an angry fit of rage. I moved in with this woman twice my age and thought I was having everything my way. I felt loved, and the sexual experience was wonderful. But in three weeks she was tired of me, so she fixed me up with another woman, then another. By the time I was nineteen, I had slept with more than thirty women.

"Then suddenly I met Jesus and everything changed. I came to this Christian university to play football, and I thought that whole chapter of my life was ended. Now, this year, I've met the woman I really want to marry. She's a beautiful and godly woman, who has no history of sexual involvement in her relationships. And I haven't been sexual with her either. But, Dr. Joy, not a week goes by that I don't sleep around on her. I cheat on her all the time and I can't get it stopped. It's killing me. Can you help me?"

There it was again—rage building toward the parents, leaving home. The experience of being used by an older woman turned into a series of sexual encounters that emptied his sense of worth. Now, Rodney's question to me was the open door to his return to wholeness: "It's killing me. Can you help me?"

ROTTEN SENSE OF SELF

The macho facade is a thin disguise of toughness that many men wear to protect themselves and keep others from discovering what empty and hurting people they really are. Those who have concluded that they have a "zero" value create an attractive but largely hollow image to hide behind. Looked at through a medical metaphor, the tough and cocky male is an artist of self-protection hiding behind emotional scar tissue. We may never learn what originally caused the wounds. But there is one thing these men learn from experience: Never be vulnerable again; never risk another deadly wound of rejection. The scar tissue also serves to mask the painful reality of low self-esteem. When the macho male does offer gestures of intimacy in what appears to be a healthy relationship, he usually keeps other relational options open as insurance against being dumped.

Such Casanovas also tend to end relationships abruptly, leaving friends, lovers, fiancées, and even spouses behind. It doesn't take an X-ray of their emotions to read shame, fear, and desperation in the guys who keep the sleeping bag rolled up behind the girl's couch, because they know they cannot establish an enduring, trusting, lifelong relationship. "I'll call," he says as he prepares to leave. But he never does. He knows when he is through, but his scarred emotions don't allow him to be honest with her and bring an orderly end to the relationship. *He* has to be the one to "dump" his partner. It would hurt too badly to go through a healthy grief over love invested and lost. Casanova is reflexively programmed to protect his deformity. One more blow, hollow as he is, might kill him.

When I had my conversation with Rodney, I had sympathetically found a way to describe the macho facade. But it took two of my students to identify and walk backward through their "macho construction" step by step and reveal their identical survival strategies—the macho mask was the product of their working very hard to survive against tragic and painful early life experiences. The building blocks of the macho facade seem to emerge in the following sequence:

1. Early devastation of the male self-esteem;
2. Making a decision to build a wall to survive;
3. Developing a self-protection strategy to guard the damaged, hollow person—facade maintenance;
4. Using anger-masked insecurity to define relationships;
5. Sabotaging potentially intimate relationships out of fear that the real, deformed self will be uncovered.

DESTRUCTION OF SELF-ESTEEM

The macho scar usually begins with some devastating wound. Typically, it is formed to protect against a previous pain or loss. Rodney's turbulent home actually drove him away in his mid-teens and into the arms of a promiscuous older woman as her "live in."

I learned more of the typical macho character during a three-way conversation with Jon and Jeff—two of my students who described their descent into successful "self protection" at a time that they could not have survived the devastation of self-respect that their families heaped on them.

Jon, youngest of three children, was the "little victim" in a divorce. Feeling abandoned by his natural father, and with his mother absorbed and troubled in a new marriage, Jon saw his stepfather as indifferent and as having stolen his mother from him. While a teenage brother and sister turned to alcohol, sex, and drugs for their "self-medication" of the lost family, Jon determined to be "a good kid" even if he had to parent himself and meet his needs alone.

I had never met Jon until a Saturday morning campus seminar on developing healthy relationships brought us together. For that seminar I worked through the childhood and teenage development needs every kid deserves to have met. At one point, I suggested that everyone close their eyes and recall the most painful loss they had experienced during childhood.

Jon told me that when he closed his eyes, he could see himself standing at the top of a cold, metal-edged stair rail in a two-story, inner-city house:

"I'm sure it isn't true, but in my memory, I can't remember my mother ever coming to the floor where our bedrooms were. I remember night after night standing at that cold and lonely spot begging Mother to come upstairs and tuck me in bed. I wanted her to hug me and hold me. But she would tell me to go to bed, that I was old enough to do that by myself. I now know that she was having trouble in her new marriage, but I couldn't understand that. I was just a child!"

Jeff's erosion of self-esteem was more subtle than Jon's. Jeff's father, a popular high school gym teacher, was friendly to everyone in the community, and especially to teens. So as Jeff grew up, he knew he needed to excel in sports to gain his father's favor. From childhood, his dad was his worst critic. Though Jeff excelled as an athlete, his father offered little positive feedback, reserving his praise for Jeff's peers. Jeff's dad would privately criticize his performance. Such humiliation was delivered to the older siblings as well. By the end of high school, Jeff was running on empty, carried a heavy countenance, and was set to strike a very effective self-protecting macho pose.

The concept, "self-respect," is poorly named, because there is almost no contribution the self can make to esteem. The role of "self" is to "construct" a feeling of value and respect or a feeling of worthlessness based on how other people treat us. A sense of worth is derived from significant relationships, interaction, and the feedback which affirms the person. Rodney received violent and negative ingredients added to his "cup of self-esteem," and he was set by the teen years to begin acting out his destructive pattern of behavior. Jon was drained of any sense of instrinsic worth, but his experience was less violent than Rodney's. Jon felt emotional bankruptcy because he wanted so much to be hugged, kissed, and supported. Jeff was caught in a double bind of being regarded as lucky to have such an affirming father, but nobody knew how shabbily his dad treated him at home.

DECISION TO SURVIVE: SELF-PROTECTION

The visible toughness of the macho male is a clue to his early decision to make it alone. The "macho scar" I am describing turns out to be only a tough mask. The scarred male usually will be crippled in his efforts to establish respect, vulnerability, or intimacy in relationships as long as the core issue of negative self-esteem remains sealed away and undisclosed. He may go through the motions of intimacy, especially sexually, but in his self-protective armor he cannot be open and vulnerable to further risk or hurt. Instead, he simply uses women as instruments of his own desire and tends to abandon them quickly when the threat of intimacy encroaches.

The bottom line is the human need to survive. Abraham Maslow has defined it as the controlling need. In a life-threatening situation, the need to stay alive takes priority over everything else. So it is not surprising that abused children, such as Rodney, often make a decision to cope—to learn to live in spite of impossible conditions of rejection, emotional deprivation, and physical violence. Infant mortality and disease cases are sometimes symptoms that a child has given up fighting against the odds. But Rodney, Jon, and Jeff were tough little survivors, so they plugged their ears and steeled themselves against painful family experiences.

Jon, sobbing in the night, gritted his teeth determined to survive his mother's emotional abandonment, loss of his natural father through divorce, and isolation from his older siblings.

Jon grieves today, "The three of us kids all tried to cope for ourselves alone. We didn't pull together. We could have survived without so much damage — and I suffered the least of the three — if we had only helped each other. Instead, we were each shattered in our own way. Crying in the night, I remember promising myself that I would be such a good boy that they would *have* to love me. I would succeed at everything I did, so they would *have* to applaud me. They'd see! I was going to be good at everything I did!"

Jeff, observing his popular father turn into a depressed and bitter husband and parent, sided with his mother, made friends with her in her own emotional anguish, and came to resent his father. He determined to survive, but had to leave the first path to manhood since his father's rejection blocked the way to simple father adoration. Jeff's decision to survive was complicated. He reckoned, "To be a man, I must be more like the man my mother deserves." It was a long road because he had to build his manhood prematurely, foreclosing part of his youth, and do it without the benefit of a positive relationship with the man everybody else admired.

ANGER: SETTING RELATIONAL BOUNDARIES
Remember that the macho personality begins with the destruction of self-esteem, leaving the young boy or teenager feeling empty. Among those who grow up coping, there is a universal core commitment to survival. So it is not surprising that most of these macho kids have told themselves that there were other people to blame for their pain. Such deep and growing resentment tends to replace the self-esteem ingredient until the inner cup is full of anger.

Jon said, "Suddenly, I realized that I had survived by protecting myself from being hurt by others. Never again would I be vulnerable. I would bump early and give the signal that 'You're not going to hurt me, so keep your distance.' I would expose a little piece of my anger very early in friendships, so they would know not to mess with me. This survival strategy became a fifteen-year rehearsal of deformed social skills that have kept me from ever letting anybody really know me."

It is typical that the macho facade man will come on strong, make a bid for attention, attract friends who admire strength, and seek to be in control. Such a facade is especially attractive to a woman who has been victimized by men in the past. Her damaged self-esteem responds almost magnetically to the macho way. In some cases, her cry seems to be for protection by a strong man. In others, she seems drawn to a damaged man against whom she can bounce her own woundedness, resentment, and anger. But the final alliance is frequently between the macho man and the damaged woman, and the hurts they sustained early in life are perpetuated in the future.

SABOTAGE: THE SELF-DESTRUCT STRATEGY

Rodney's voluntary confession to me was a rare move for a man with a macho facade. Indeed that initiative means that the facade is softening at the edges.

"I don't need that stuff!" or "Maybe other guys are empty, but not me!" are standard denial responses. For them, the relationship games go on. Several special strategies are practiced. Men in the grip of the macho self-protective facade tend to use them:

The arm's length seduction. The macho male is the master of tremendous first impressions. Singles bars abound with these playful, superficial, and self-protecting flirtations and introductions. They are meant to bait and titillate. An honest relationship is the last thing on the macho man's mind. Instead, he goes for the party, for the hype, for the entertainment blitz, even for the one-night stand in a sexual encounter. If he does move that far, the arm's length behavior is endlessly and artfully executed. The affair goes through the gestures of intimacy, but no attachment occurs. If it does begin to form and vulnerability emerges, the macho facade sends another message: Escape! "Don't call me. I'll call you," is a typical farewell.

He leaves one-night stands and brief romantic escapades

with a promise to be in touch. This rarely occurs because maintenance of the facade demands that he shuck off this close brush with vulnerability and move into safer encounters. In a very brief time, the facade scar thickens and self-protection desensitizes the original vision of vulnerability and intimacy. He quickly develops compensating strategies for getting sexual contact, even if it must be without permanence and lifelong commitment. He becomes skilled in using the tricks of seduction. He can tell a dozen or hundred women, "I never loved anybody like I love you." Without intending to lie, he has become a compulsive con artist. He has fallen into regularly rehearsed scenarios in which "use and abandonment" are practiced with finesse and skill. Our hollow man is moving on a one-way road into the ultimate isolation.

At one level, the machismo's friends and lovers are often ready to do him violence. But at another level, it is important to remember the loneliness and isolation he experiences if we cannot bring him to integrity and honesty. This original and tender vision of an exclusive lifelong relationship, when exploded, may simply hurt so much that the macho facade is rolled into place as a denial mechanism. This denial is an essential anesthetic for continuing through the magnetic social patterns which promise sexual expression sooner or later. And with the macho man, it is almost always "sooner," because he protects himself against his own vulnerability to love. He can execute the sexual transaction for simple animal pleasure, and depart emotionally unscathed in an arm's length seduction.

The bump-back approach. In virtually every relationship, the scarred macho man keeps his options open by keeping distance. It is no mystery that women who have encountered such a man often suffer a devastating blow to their self-respect. Even if she was whole and healthy when she fell into his arms, she later finds herself bumped back, reduced to an emotional wreck. And if she neglects to get her sense of wellness back, and strays into the singles scene, she is likely to be an even more striking target than before for other predator males. A striking finding in the study of rape victims tells us that women raped as girls are more likely to be raped and raped repeatedly as adults. No one can say for certain what the trigger is, but at some deep intuitive level, we may accurately read the "empty" and "abused" labels on each other's foreheads. Indeed, Aldonza's cynical lines from *Man of La Mancha* are the wail of many women who have tangled with the macho facade: "One pair of arms is like another! They're all the same!" Devastated by his exploitation, her self-respect has been reduced to match his own emptiness.

Projecting self-contempt on others. The macho's own low self-respect often gets pitched in the face of friends and lovers. It is as if his cup of self-respect is filled with mud. He has plugged the emotional wells which might have welcomed genuine intimacy. Obscenities, accusations of infidelity, and hostile assaults tell you what is inside the speaker more than anything else. Jesus once said, "Out of the abundance of the heart the mouth speaks" (Matt. 12:34). So if the affective center of life is full of junk, the mouth is going to spew it all over the place. It is important to listen with one ear toward Jesus. Remember that the scarred man is dying on the inside, and wants real intimacy more than anything in the world. But he has developed a strategy by which he at the same time:

1. Protects his damaged self-esteem by keeping friends, especially women, at arm's length;

2. Deliberately sabotages the relationship while blaming others for being inadequate, unworthy, or imperfect in some trivial way;

3. In all probablity, has also developed a compensatory strategy by which he has already established another option to which he can turn, secure in knowing he has devastated the other person first, and has avoided being dumped.

In this chapter I have presented what I have learned from young men who have trusted me with their stories about the development of the macho scar. They have shown you the high cost of those self-protecting strategies. Their stories differ from those of millions of men hardened by early or late experiences, in that they chose not to live out their lives in splendid isolation. Their first step toward reconstruction was to tell the painful story of abandonment, abuse, and their invented strategies of survival—self-protection.

The truth is a man may marry, have a good relationship, be reasonably faithful at a technical level, and be dying on the inside. If he has few friends, cannot laugh at himself, and seems edgy or defensive on a regular basis, you can be sure he is hiding something. He is dying of the internal leprosy of isolation.

The picture of a tough and lonely stag, his years of successful dominance in the herd behind him as he wanders off, alone, to die, is an image to evoke our grief. Even in those species where competitive breeding necessarily isolates the powerful and solitary male, such loneliness is a mark of a fallen and broken universe. But it is intolerable in the human community where the first principle is that "it is not good for the human to be alone." Solitary confinement, the prison system's penultimate punishment, is a Siberian exile experience, whether we are in a family, a marriage, or a community.

Do-It-Yourself Tips

Open your appointment book or grab an index card. List the girls and women who have taken you seriously and whom you dropped, dumped, abandoned, or otherwise treated shabbily. Use code names or initials and put them on a time line.

Now, separately, list the other men who know these facts about you and know your own feelings of regret about how you treated girls and women as you were finding your way as a man.

Or do this: List the names or initials of "tournament men" you have know since school days. Do the same for "macho" damaged men.

Can you celebrate your own or some of their recoveries into healthy men? Do you know friends who would benefit from being part of a Christian support group who can offer God's grace and forgiveness and healing to them? Do *you* need support? Phone me any night at 606/858-3817 and I'll help you identify network possibilities right where you live.

Contractor's Crew Notes

See whether everybody can distinguish between a "tournament" male who mixes competition with scoring and a "macho" male who is profoundly insecure and masks it with a facade of overdone marks of super masculinity. If so, get your own story on the line and then invite others to share theirs:

"As I look back at the tournament and macho symptoms I've had, I can see the most painful point for me was when. . . ."

Huddle up your "men under construction" for prayer.

CHAPTER EIGHT

MELTDOWN: RECOVERING SECURITY

I grew up among scarred and insecure boys who were abusive, distant, and threatening to their less damaged peers.

By the time I qualified for the U.S. Navy V-12 training program and was in college a year ahead of schedule on its accelerated officer training program, I was no longer afraid of these tough guys. And on campus, I found that the damaged, hurting young students seemed willing to expose their pain to me.

Indeed, after the first year of college, I was elected student body president in a sometimes rowdy political campaign. The campaign was engineered by the tough and cool guys on campus. I suspect now that I was the only outsider who knew their feelings of helplessness and inferiority. One by one these guys, some of them recently returned veterans from Word War II, would pour out their stories to me. Their fierce loyalty got me elected over the standard nominee of the incumbent campus leaders, supported by college faculty and administration. For reasons which I may not yet have fully unscrambled, these campus rejects trusted me with confidential reports on their past and present troubles. I connected some of them to Jesus in profound and transforming conversions. I discovered recently through a round of fortieth anniversary reunions that many of these once insecure and compensatory males are today my lifelong advocates in highly effective careers. Most are honest men, no longer plagued by the fears that haunted their younger years.

But not until past my sixtieth birthday did I begin to unravel the actual interior structure of the macho facade. I did this through the help of the two students I introduced in chapter 7. Jon and Jeff, the young seminarians whose journeys were quite unknown to each other, were members of the same weekly "contractor's crew network" with me. This chapter will be built around their description of the lonely world of self-protection. You will discover how they made the frightening entry into the world of vulnerability, which is essential for establishing the integrity and intimacy that males in the third decade of life need so desperately.

GETTING IN TOUCH WITH THE LITTLE BOY

JEFF: "I think I made a breakthrough this afternoon talking with my roommate. Woody is a special and faithful friend. When he offered to talk to Lucy, I knew I could trust him. So he went to tell her that I needed to be away from the relationship for a while, that I was working on some things. I feel so sorry for Lucy, because I just can't shake my negative reactions. And although we are going to be married in six weeks, more and more I just want to run away.

"Woody asked me to describe what had happened over the weekend when Lucy and I went to vist in her parents' home in Tennessee. So I told him. It was a little thing, but Lucy scolded me for something I was doing as we were riding in her dad's new pickup. I went silent. I just shut down. I wanted to leave. I always seem to want to run away when anyone criticizes me. It must be my special strategy for coping with feelings of shame and worthlessness. Lucy complains about that — suddenly I will clam up and cut everything short and just go away. And she's right. That's what I do.

"So as I was describing all of this to Woody, I said the strangest thing, 'But I'm just a little kid.' I couldn't believe my ears. Here I was describing what had happened last weekend. I am twenty-three years old. Yet that's what I said — like

I had gone crazy or something. I'm a full-grown man, and I said, 'I'm just a little kid.'

"I called this kind of a breakthrough, because talking with Woody, I suddenly saw something—the way I coped with my dad's abuse when I was young. I would leave the house. Or, I would grab things for overnight and go stay with my grandparents who lived nearby. I'm still trying to run away, and I'm a full-grown man. I went through fifteen roommates, and broke two engagements while I was in college. And I still have this flight impulse. I abandon people instead of risking being hurt again."

DON: "It's the little boy in you that wants to run away, but your commitment to Lucy and your clear perception of her as a worthy person make you know you want to marry her. You seem to have a scared little boy in you as well as a competent and basically healthy adult."

JEFF: "That's it. But I can't get the two separated, and the scared little boy takes over."

DON: "I once referred a student to Dr. John Parks, a psychiatrist in Lexington, who helped him to cope with episodes of emotional abuse in his childhood. Will's mother frequently punished him by locking him in his bedroom. He couldn't get out, and he would panic. Later, his interpersonal relationships showed traces of a compulsive clinging for security, evidently out of fear of being punished or abandoned. One day when Will was very depressed he stopped by my office. He seemed dangerously depressed, so I phoned Dr. Parks, reported what I was seeing, and suggested that Will might need medication to be stabilized. The doctor phoned the Wilmore drugstore, and Will went to pick up the medication. He was back in twenty minutes to show me the label. Dr. Parks had prescribed the medication for 'Willy,' not for William or Will. We laughed together in a wonderful moment of insight. It was the little boy's insecurity, not Will's adult panic that needed the treatment."

JEFF: "I notice that I always identify with the underdog in movies and on television. I think most viewers identify with the winners, but there I go off into the shadows with the person who is being abused and destroyed. It is like there is this little Jeff inside me who shrivels up when anything goes wrong or someone gives negative feedback. Little Jeff feels like he can never do anything right, and he wants to run away when things go wrong. He feels helpless and worthless."

DON: "But the adult Jeff that I know is a reliable, productive person—always on time with assignments, radiantly handsome, and calm."

JEFF: "I know. That is the way I really am, except when something drops me back into my little Jeff."

DON: "Will you let me give you permission to comfort little Jeff? It would mean that it is OK to say to him that whatever he is feeling is all right. You would never have made it to adulthood in such good shape if he hadn't learned to cope by running away from the abuse.

"You can tell Lucy that you are working on little Jeff's fears and hurts, but that it is not her problem. You are OK as a man. Your problems are not about her, or even about you. They are about things that happened to you long ago. Tell her you want the little boy to find healing and security, so you can be a healthy and playful adult."

JEFF: "When I feel afraid and vulnerable, how can I keep little Jeff separate from my own adult self?"

DON: "Try talking to the frightened and damaged little boy. When you are alone and you feel pangs of panic and insecurity and want to run away from something, separate out the frightened little Jeff. Look into your bathroom mirror for example and see him behind the adult eyes in front of you. Or cradle an extra pillow in your arms and cry at night, comforting little Jeff. Thank him for taking good care of himself and doing what he knew he had to do to survive. Tell him he was a good kid.

"As you talk to little Jeff, you'll bring healing to him and these reflexive emotional flashbacks will leave you. What you are doing is grieving. A good grief always takes a long time, but it is worth it because it brings healing, wholeness, and integrity. I know you as a tender, sensitive, and gracious adult. I know that you needed a different kind of parenting than you got, especially from your critical and abusive father. What he did might have worked well with another kid, but it was painful and abusive to you. So welcome to the world of your own healing."

RECOGNIZING THE MACHO SYMPTOMS

Jeff's crisis revolved around the fact that he found himself damaging his engagement. He told how his engagement almost ended when he resorted to bickering with and criticizing his fiancée. When he finally succeeded in offending her, she would strike back with words that drove him down into depression and self-annihilating abandonment.

"Slowly, I began to see that I was imitating how my father treated my mother. I hated the way he treated her, yet here I was doing the same thing. It was ironic that I had rejected that way of relating, yet I seemed doomed to repeat it."

Jeff, entirely alone, was able to recognize and report his discovery about his macho damage. Jon, in contrast, had been "doing his own surgery" in our family room, with great agony. Then, an amazing moment exploded in my office during a support network session over lunch. As Jeff began to give us the play-by-play account of his solitary breakthrough—much as it is recounted here—Jon's eyes widened and he shot a knowing glance to me across the room. He couldn't wait to blurt out his own exactly parallel story. When Jeff finished describing the shabby treament he was giving his fiancée, Jon illustrated how he was taking his unresolved anger against his mother and dumping it on Arla.

"The closer I got to Arla the worse I treated her," Jon complained. "I can't believe how negative I was. In my mind I would criticize her for everything. I would tear her apart inside my head—worried that she dressed too provocatively. I even questioned her spiritual maturity. She was too emotional and not logical enough. Everything about her seemed to bother me. Me, for pity's sake, with all of my junk and failures. Who was I to be criticizing her? I was a jerk! Here I was projecting all of my own insecurity and shame on to her!"

DISSOLVING THE FACADE

Working occasionally with Jon across a six-month period in reconstructing his interior "little boy" damage showed me an X-ray image of the macho facade. And the most telling insight came through his tears.

"This is such a familiar territory to me. I have been using my own hurt ever since I was a little boy. It hurt when people didn't meet my needs. I determined to keep people far enough away so that I couldn't ever be hurt again as I was in growing up and crying myself to sleep."

Jon told how he had successfully sabotaged dozens of friendships, and two or three prize romantic possibilities. "I was skilled at using mildly offensive strategies, often masked in humor, to put people on their guard. It was as if I had found a way to keep them off-balance, so if the relationship turned sour, I could walk away and blame it on them. I was so fragile I knew I couldn't bear to hurt anymore, so I kept my dukes up and bumped them away."

Jon's breakthrough ushered in a season of grieving for the "bump back" strategy he had used for the last sixteen years. He took the time to walk through an inventory of faithful friends he had "bumped" so he could protect himself and walk away with no emotional risks.

TO LOVE, OR NOT?

As Jon and Jeff continued their recap of the spring's break-through and the new confidence they were both enjoying, I turned to Jeff.

DON: "Jeff, you're so gentle. You sneaked up on us in the support group Tuesday. Nobody was prepared for the bomb you dropped. You should see Jon work on this stuff. He yells and sweats. Twice Robbie and I have seen him reduced to what looked like involuntary muscular seizures as he appears to wrestle with himself. The first time he went into this kind of seizure I wondered whether I should call 911. How did you work through dissolving your self-protection?"

JEFF: "The breakthrough came, as I told you. It was the Tuesday after the weekend I had worked through some real struggles with Lucy. I was finding that I could not open my-self up to anybody—even to Lucy—in a deep way. So after my solitary weekend, we went out to eat on Thursday.

"I told her, 'I don't know what's wrong. I know it's not you. There's something I've got to break through.' I had come to this point in relationships before, when I would start finding things wrong with the person. I'd say to myself, 'This is too close. I can't handle this.' Then I would go on into another relationship.

"I told you I went through fifteen roommates in college. I would soon find something wrong with each of them. I wouldn't let them get close to me, and I would not want to get too close to them. But I never realized what was happen-ing until my relationship with Lucy. I was going to have to be vulnerable to Lucy or break this relationship. I was going to have to let her know my secrets—everything. It was almost as if I was trying to criticize her enough to push her away, make her abandon me."

DON: "What was it that you saw you had to break through?"

JEFF: "It was my terrible fear of being hurt—rejected—by somebody if I let them close to me. I didn't trust Lucy. I think I saw that it was my fear that created the barrier. To be sure I wouldn't be the one hurt, I would begin criticizing and keep her from getting close. It was my way of avoiding hurt."

JON: "Wow! Just last summer I stepped out on Arla to keep an option open in case she dumped me. Here we were en-gaged, and I asked another woman out for a date! How sick! All I was doing was playing games that guaranteed to keep me from getting close to anybody."

JEFF: "I can understand that. What helped me get through this was my commitment to Lucy. My feelings were totally out of the picture by this time. I operated on a decision I made to break the intimacy barrier."

DON: "What was the commitment made of if the feelings were gone?"

JEFF: "It was a commitment to work through whatever was damaging our relationship. I strongly sensed that God wanted us to be together. So I decided I simply had to learn to trust her."

DON: "By this time you were engaged, weren't you? How did you work through the lack of trust—the fear of vulnerability?"

JEFF: "I sat in my room all weekend. I prayed. I asked Lucy for some time away—to be alone to objectively look at our relationship somehow. I started reading Dr. Larry Crabb's book, *Inside Out.*"[1]

DON: "What changed in your perception of yourself during the weekend? Anything?"

JEFF: "What I saw was that I didn't have the capacity to love Lucy. I was preoccupied with protecting all of my own feelings of shame and inferiority—all that negative stuff. And I knew that's not love, at least not by the definitions in 1 Corinthians 13."

DON: "Did it ever occur to you, Jeff, that this negative material might be coming out of your feelings of being abused by your father? When I first met you, you were struggling with feelings of agnosticism. You said you couldn't pray. You felt worthless. Yet, neither you nor Jon looks like a candidate for low self-esteem. You are both good looking and intelligent men. So, I never would have thought to ask about deep feelings of hunger for worth, self-respect, competency, and confidence. In fact, you may remember that I asked about your relationship with your father, since that is such a crucial predictor of problems with prayer and religious belief.

"Men with unfinished business with their fathers tend to flirt with total agnosticism about God or at least to experience 'prayer paralysis.' This was my hunch when you first came to me to talk about your inability to pray. You see, if your dad is rejecting you, he is the 'image of God' to you, and that is enough to shut down your praying, because it says you aren't worth listening to. It is low self-esteem of the most personal and spiritual sort. I wasn't surprised to see that same sense of insecurity and inferiority damaging your relationship with friends and now with Lucy.

"See, if you were down on yourself, you would reflect that

negativism onto your closest relationships. If you feel worthless, you will need to bring the other person down to the same level."

JON: "That's interesting. Unbelievable, what a perspective!"

JEFF: "I think the breakthrough was learning that God truly did love me."

CAN LOVE BE REAL?

JON: "How in the world am I going to be able to love Arla? I'm not a good lover. I'm not healthy, Jeff. And I hear you saying the same thing about your relationship to Lucy."

DON: "What does a good lover do?"

JON: "A good lover focuses on strengths and encourages the person. I said originally that I needed her or enjoyed her, but love her? Loving means if she gets burned and her face is scarred, I am going to be with her. Right now, I know Arla loves me and I wonder if that's why I love her? Do I just love her back?

"I just want to be sure I've got the right kind of love to make this work, because I've never been able to really love anyone before. I've never given my heart to someone before, never been committed to loving anyone just for their own sake before."

DON: "Let me remind you guys that you are the resident authorities on the macho syndrome. The one characteristic of the syndrome you have been defining is the inability to be truly vulnerable, to risk loving even when exposed to the threat of being hurt.

"There is another characteristic that I see now and then. These kinds of males tend to be competitive, falling into the pattern of the imperfectly bonding male."

I described for them the tournament male discussed in chapter 6. These showy and competitive men tend to develop harems—all at once, or one at a time if they can't get away with polygamy. They are always "looking," constantly trying to figure out how to attract and support additional females. This is true in the animal kingdom as well as among humans.

These males have wandering eyes. Instead of investing the enormous energy it takes to live honestly and vulnerably with one woman, they live superficially with many. They try to minimize their risks by secretly maintaining multiple relationships. But the tournament male inevitably becomes like the legendary lonely and solitary stag who goes into exile to die alone.

JON: "Does that change the roles, then, for a human male, if he repudiates being a tournament type?"

DON: "It means that we've got to put down our fallen nature. All males are fallen—sons of Adam! It calls for a slow and deliberate pair bonding schedule. It shows up as fathers make a high investment in the care of the young. It means that the sacrifical husband who lays down his life for his wife is going against the grain of human nature."

JON: "What does it mean for a man to lay down his life for his wife?"

DON: "Well, it means, at least, you're always vulnerable. There are no secrets. 'Naked and unashamed' means everything is a risk."

JEFF: "Always vulnerable. Wow."

DON: "You can see what vulnerability through your new-found security will do for you. It means you now have the courage to be intentional. Intimacy is the name of this marriage. You don't have any secrets to hide. There is nothing you could not own, because you have built unconditional trust in this relationship. You lay down everything."

JEFF: "That's scary, though! Do you know how scary that is for the first-timer?"

DON: "But you are already finding out how rewarding it is."

JEFF: "Yeah. I've never felt better now that I've decided to break down the wall."

DON: "And it will only get better."

JEFF: "But what if the old fears come back and I feel like running away, maybe after we are married?"

DON: "They *will* return. You can count on that, but you have broken the power of those old fears. Now you can take Lucy with you and revisit the old experiences, even carry on a dialogue with the insecure and frightened little Jeff. This is sort of retroactive healing, as you walk down painful memories with someone who knows, understands, and loves you."

SELFISHNESS OR GENUINE CONCERN?
JON: "I've got this selfish, self-righteous something inside of me. I'm doing great because I'm doing such a good job of getting healed. Isn't that sad that I'm so self-centered?"

DON: "Sure, Jon's doing it, healing himself."

JON: "Isn't that sad that I think that way? It's pathetic."

DON: "But you told us recently in the support group, that on numerous occasions, in class or during chapel, you've been so overwhelmed by peace and love that your eyes have filled with tears. You are simply celebrating God's faithfulness to you. When you acknowledge Him, you know then that you are not riding on your own self-will or resting on your own goodness."

JON: "I know it is God's grace in those fleeting moments. I feel so grateful. But how can I go from so much love, and so much respect for Arla, to suspecting that it's all emotions and not real? I say to myself, 'Let's get this straight, Jon! We're talking fifty years here, and you better be sure on this one.' I struggle between going back into my negativism and what is legitimate questioning and responsibility."

DON: "Those are likely the reasons why our culture developed the pre-engagement and engagement stages. During that time a couple can make a responsible evaluation. You can sort out your feelings about engagement, marriage, family, and the rest of your life. But the conscious surrender of your motivations to God's cleansing and empowering grace will give you a perspective from which to look at your relationship with Arla and to keep it transparent and honest. Now that you have taken care of little Jon's fears and insecurities, you can be vulnerable to any truth about yourself."

ONE PATH TO WHOLENESS
I continue to be amazed at how clear it is. The macho male has adopted his facade of competence and smoothness as a

survival strategy and a mask to hide his insecurity and inferiority. Thus, we can understand that the key to dissolving this handsome, often stunningly attractive macho mask requires working backward through the same sequence of four steps. Remember the four steps involved:

1. Destruction of your self-respect.
2. Your self-protection and facade construction.
3. Your anger-masked protection from further hurt.
4. Your pattern of sabotaging relationships.

The best path to recovery that I have observed requires beginning with the last step and climbing up to the final repair of self-esteem. It looks, then, like this:

1. Acknowledge that you are your own worst enemy. Your strategies of "self protection" are isolating you and starving you to death for honesty, trust, and intimacy in any relationship. This "confession" is the toughest of all of the steps of recovery and transformation, because it means admitting that your survival strategy which has "worked" for you is also destroying you. I told Jon one night during a painful "surgical" session, "You likely wouldn't have made it if you hadn't hardened your heart to people. It was your survival strategy. But it is what is now turning you into a lonely man. It is time to let the strategy go."

2. Defuse the "anger" explosives with which you "bumped back and protected yourself" from people who could hurt you. See whether you can go back to a primary "stressor" from whom you protected yourself as the earliest means of survival. Sort out what was your responsibility and what you must release to the people who were spilling their agendas all over your early life.

Recently I offered to interview on tape a man who was unable to write well enough to ventilate his lifelong resentment. We then made a cassette tape book, which we called, "The Story of My Early Life." The book of tapes became his permanent record of the abuse and humiliation he endured in his childhood.

3. Decide to be vulnerable again, now that you have managed to survive an emotional holocaust. Own your feelings of anger or inferiority that have fueled your macho self-protection. Name it as a "self-protecting" strategy. "It is my problem, not yours!" is a good beginning line in a genuine apology for sabotaging a friendship. If the first rule is that "feelings are OK," then the second rule must follow quickly: "It is my junk. I cannot justify dumping it on you. I don't like myself after I've done it. Please forgive me. I want to stop doing it." You cannot be a friend or love another until you befriend yourself. You can love others only to the extent that you love yourself.

The Jesus axiom is deadly as well as wonderful. It is a terrible thing to "love your neighbor as yourself" if you are running on empty, packed with emotional mud where self-respect should have filled the cup. If you are desperate, violent, and a saboteur of relationships, then others will certainly wish that you would not "love" them too much!

4. Refill the cup of self-esteem. Separate out the "little boy," the "wounded child," or the "devastated teenager" in you from the present man of integrity you have become through God's transforming grace. Tell the little boy, for example, "You did a good job. You were just a child and it was not your fault that bad things happened to you. You are a survivor. So it's OK to hurt, to cry, and to scream. But I am here to protect you, and I've got wisdom and energy now to guarantee that you are safe. So let me take care of you."

If your memories are more visual than verbal, let your mind take you back to the most painful memory of your devastated period of life. Frame that picture as if you were looking at it on TV, watching the humiliation and the heroics you performed to survive. While the image is at maximum power, create another parallel picture of you as you are now, with your present wisdom, integrity, and ability to cope with that long-past tragic episode still on your other memory "screen." Go one step further and say, "If I could revisit the scene, this is what I would say, do, and feel as I delivered that young boy out of the jaws of humiliation and destruction." As this healthy and mature image dominates, you will have "separated" your childhood from your present. And, wonderful reality, you will be equipping yourself to be God's agent of deliverance for other helpless people as they are being exploited, abandoned, or abused.

Give yourself permission, too, to accept the feedback, the affection, and the unconditional positive regard that comes from other people who know your whole story and steadily value you. You are now refilling your cup of self-respect with the most precious and indestructible fuel for healthy behavior known on earth—you are loved!

For those of us who care about men's continuing construction of healthy masculinity, the hardest part is often to accept their statement that "the problem is my own, not yours." But to find healing, they will need faithful friends and spouses, not "rescuers." God's reconstructive grace requires that the victims accept God's empowering to do the hard work of memory and reconstruction themselves. The macho facade must be abolished by the man himself. We can affirm our unwavering commitment, but the work must be done by these heroic survivors.

RECOVERING FROM SEXUAL ADDICTION

Neither Jon nor Jeff had been promiscuous. While they had sabatoged relationships that left a series of women bewildered, they had not left human wreckage in their wakes. Rodney, whose story of promiscuity opened chapter 7, was a love-bandit who could not get his promiscuity stopped—not even when he had found Christian conversion and had located the Christian woman of his dreams.

"There is not a week that goes by," he confessed to me, "that I don't sleep around and cheat on her, and we've never gotten sexual at all. How can I get this stopped?" So, there is a deeper recovery that many "love-them-and-leave-them" men need.

Earlier in this book I set down the amazing facts about male sexuality and development which make young men profoundly vulnerable to compulsive sexual activity:

1. Male sexuality is hormonally charged, and
2. His fertility is "locked in" to the highest pleasure.

3. His sexual anatomy is the basic affirmation of his male identity, but
4. His sexuality is shrouded in privacy and secrecy
5. As preparation for "presentation" to his exclusive life-long woman—his wife.
6. Since male sex is highly charged and profoundly personal and private,
7. Most males do not develop language and basic knowledge which is constructive, rich, and ennobling to this best gift of their personhood.
8. So the typical male lives in embarrassed "denial" of his need for tenderness and meaning, and indulges in secret, embarrassing, but titillating sexual experiences which leave his deepest needs frustrated and wrapped in further humiliation and shame.

Any man who examines how his sexual energy has been expressed is looking at high-voltage resources that could have been diverted into compulsive, self-gratifying behaviors. In an environment of accountability, most men can come to terms with their imagination and sexual behavior and find that it loses its compulsive, driven characteristics. Compulsive behavior follows a pattern that is secretly launched by a powerful, often trancelike desire. [Watch this "cycle" of compulsive sexual addiction on the circular diagram on page 152.]

If the behavior is not intercepted during the desire phase, it moves into an almost hypnotically carried out ritual, developed because it delivers the payoff episode (food, sex, alcohol, drugs, power, exhilaration). The episode is the climax event, followed by feelings of shame—humiliation, depression, and failure. Most people with one compulsive addiction have two or three, so when they are depressed over one failure, they often "kick in" another trancelike preoccupation and are off on a second Ferris wheel ride of "trance-ritual-episode-shame."

Many of us began our compulsive behaviors in innocence, often in "initiation rites" administered by our peer deities. Yet those rituals, demanded as admission tickets by the "cool crowd," left us running on empty from the first episode.

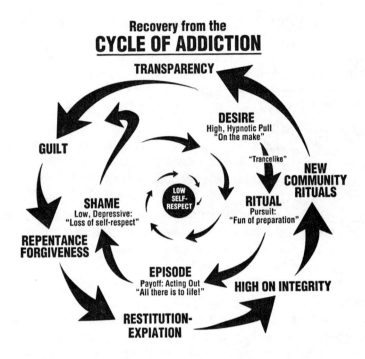

Recovery from the
CYCLE OF ADDICTION

Others found their sexual addiction triggered by a devastating catalytic environment or event. The catalytic environment most often turns out to have been during our childhood. Any situation in which shame engulfs us puts us at major risk. So if we are berated, humiliated, abused, or isolated and emotionally abandoned as children, our compulsive addictions are our "self-medication"—our way of finding comfort, distraction, or relief from the shame we feel as victims. When significant adults do not maintain an orderly, predictable, and safe environment, or where marital stress, alcoholism, family separation, divorce, or abuse is present you can count on it: they have created an atmosphere in which compulsive behavior can be spawned.

However, the compulsive behavior rarely becomes visible until the onset of pubescence. This is true even though sexual compulsiveness is not part of the "self-medication." Turning to alcohol, vandalism, violence, burglary, or street drugs is a common symptom of deep, shame-driven addiction. And shame is the motor which drives the behavior, producing more humiliation in an increasing crescendo, cycle after cycle.

It is shame, not guilt, which burrows a black hole in the personality, as compulsive behavior digs a deeper and deeper pit of negative self-judgments. Shame builds more privacy and more careful rituals, until in final desperation it may drive the person either toward self-destruction or taking a flagrant public risk, in the attempt to destroy the marriage and family.

Shame consists of a cluster of narcissistic wounds: feelings of humiliation, fear of discovery, public embarrassment, inadequacy, and of being a sham. Shame further erodes self-confidence, makes integrity a mere phantom, and requires effective cover-up to function in the family and in public. It provides no basis for recovery and rehabilitation, or redemption and forgiveness. When shame is finally tracked down and caught, it refuses to disclose the full pattern of destructive behavior and history of failure. Inevitably, it is willing only to deal with what has been publicly exposed.

Guilt, on the other hand, consists of owning full responsibliity for behavior and for the history of failure. Guilt motors a full and good confession and is eager to get the whole load of past failure and private misdeeds named and owned. It rarely blames other people, even though an objective judge would find that responsibility should be shared among others.

If someone will locate us in our pit of shame following yet another episode, or if we can pay attention to our "Desire," no matter how faint it is, to take responsibility for our failures, then "Shame" can be transformed into "Guilt." Guilt, then, is able to start us toward making a full and complete disclosure in the ears of supportive people. "Forgiveness" comes through this honest confession. The exhilaration of recovery empowers us to make "Restitution" or "Expiation" — paying for our past failures to people we have hurt and wronged. This sets off a new "High on Integrity," establishing a "New Ritual" of honesty and vulnerability, and a life of "Transparency" in the new and trusted community.

When a man can identify his own compulsive tendencies and name them among a group of peers in a support environment, the addiction cycle can be broken. Patrick Carnes has identified a "Twelve Step" program for supporting people who are recovering from sexual addiction. It is outlined in his book, *Out of the Shadows: Understanding Sexual Addiction.*[2]

Dozens of groups now use Twelve Step recovery programs, most of them following the famous Alcoholic Anonymous sequence first generated by Dr. Sam Shoemaker and the Moral Rearmament Movement. But an almost identical recovery program existed in John Wesley's "Penitent Bands" in mid-1700s England. Wesley found that converts who were given "tickets" admitting them to the "United Societies" and the "Class Meeting" turned out to have serious compulsive behavior problems. These were detected in the home visits of the "Class Leader." While all members of Societies and Classes were invited to a voluntary spiritual support network called "Bands," those who were faltering in their life of obedience to God were referred to "Penitent Bands." The rules were simple:

1. Meet together to confess their faults and to pray for one another that they may be healed.
2. Societies and Classes must be divided into several bands, to consist of not fewer than five nor more than ten persons.
3. The band leader will interrogate the others, in sequence, meeting on Monday nights and one additional time convenient to all each week.
4. Everyone will speak as freely, plainly, and concisely as possible, the real state of the heart, citing each instance of temptation and deliverance since the last meeting.
5. Exactly at 10 o'clock at night, if the business is not finished, a short prayer be offered and the meeting ended with the sharing to continue at the next appointed meeting.
6. Each person will stand while speaking and no one may speak until that person sits down.
7. Nothing mentioned in the band meeting may be men-

tioned by anyone outside of the meeting.

8. If any person misses a meeting without an extraordinary reason, that person will be privately confronted. If there is a second absence, the matter will be discussed with the person before the entire band.

The Penitent Bands observed the same rules as Bands and Classes, but Penitent meetings almost always were held on the nights of their greatest compulsive vulnerability. Many met on Saturday nights and took on such character of a "party" and ran so late that Wesley was criticized by other Methodists for permitting the long and late Penitent Band meetings. He noted that they were using energy that had long been used for evil purposes, and did not discourage these recovery groups of his.[3]

My own great grandfather, W.W. Hulet, was a Band worker in the late 1800s, given by God a heart for the poor and disenfranchised. Although he established Societies and Classes in six states, he always had time for visiting the saloon district of Kansas City when he returned home to his family after traveling and preaching in the Western territories. He died on the streets in front of those saloons, evidently from a stroke or heart attack, but sadly assumed by passersby to be a drunk (although he was dressed in his typical preaching coat and suit). So, as a tribute to W.W. Hulet and his calling as a Free Methodist evangelist in the John Wesley spirit, I offer my own Wesleyanized Penitent Band version of the Twelve Steps as they seem to have been practiced by Wesley and Hulet. I use them today with men's groups (see page 156).

In *Re-bonding: Preventing and Restoring Damaged Relationships,* I explore additional steps for healing from broken relationships, especially where adultery and promiscuity have been involved.[4] The recovery support group pattern needs to be maintained over a minimum of one year of faithful weekly sessions, to predict significant stabilization and the ability to cope without group accountability. But every man needs lifelong significant support in an intentional network simply to remain a healthy and growing person.

Twelve Steps for Penitent Men

1. We admitted that we were powerless over our compulsive behavior—that our lives had become unmanageable, and we voluntarily reached out to trusted people for help.
2. We came to see that God mediates His grace through trusted people who listen unconditionally, offer forgiveness, demand accountability, and walk with us in the redeeming community of Jesus.
3. Thus forgiven, accountable, and affirmed, we accepted God's sanctifying grace with its day-by-day cleansing of our thoughts, words, relationships, and behaviors.
4. We wrote a searching and fearless moral inventory of our past behavior and addiction, both reducing the past to an objective record to free our subjective consciences, and providing an agenda for restitution and sacrificial reconciliation.
5. We appealed for divine forgiveness by confessing responsibility for our behavior to God and by naming the exact nature of our wrongs to a support group spiritual director with whom we shared our inventory of past failure and addiction.
6. We surrendered our attachment to those addictive behaviors and asked God to heal all of these present defects of character, as well as to heal their roots and traces throughout our past lives.
7. We humbly asked God to remove our shortcomings and our tendencies to drift into isolation and into compulsive behavior.
8. We made a list of all persons we had harmed and became willing to make amends to them all.
9. We made direct restitution to all people we had wronged wherever possible, except when our network support group advised us that to do so would have injured them or other people.
10. We continue to take personal inventory and when we are wrong promptly admit it and acknowledge that we are continually recovering from our past deformities.
11. We are seeking through prayer and meditation to improve our conscious contact with God, seeking for knowledge to know His will for us and for the power to carry that out.
12. Having had a profound moral and spiritual renewal as a result of these steps, we are trying to carry this message of hope and healing to others and to practice these principles in all of our activities.

In this chapter, you have listened to two recovering macho men. As a subset of the larger species of tournament males, they may have revealed some symptoms that help you to understand yourself or someone of importance to you. Most of all, the bold honesty of Jon and Jeff is a model for all of us who long to be people of integrity in the outer world and who are willing to go "inside out." I also reacquainted you with Rodney, who discovered that he couldn't stop his promiscuous tendencies even after he became a Christian. So I offered you the recovery strategy, rooted in John Wesley's Penitent Bands and in Sam Shoemaker's Twelve Step model, as a tough but rewarding journey to integrity and a new ritual of holy, healthy living. There is life after devastation!

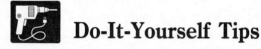 **Do-It-Yourself Tips**

Use your photo album or other strategy of revisiting your childhood and teen years. Do you want to congratulate the "little Jon or Jeff" from your childhood? Think of your present self as "built up" emotionally much like a giant tree. The early years remain at the center of that trunk. Similarly, your "little Joe or Jim or Jack" is still is there. Try talking to him about his good show as a kid, his courage, his survival capacity when bad things were dumped on him at school or on the street—or even at home as Jon and Jeff experienced.

Then, try to imagine Jesus picking up a young child and holding him while talking to his parents and other significant adults in his life. Can you let Jesus pick up your little boy, accept him, affirm him, and even warn the adults in his life not to let any harm come to him? Try blessing your own childhood.

Contractor's Crew Notes

Open the door for your crew to dip into their own "little boy" memories. Lead off, and give each man a choice of a story to tell:

1. "I hid my secrets, too, much as Jeff did, and it showed up when. . . ."

2. "I felt emotionally abused or at least damaged as a kid when. . . ."

3. "The way I finally became willing to be vulnerable to my wife, to God, and to you guys came about because. . . ."

Read Matthew 18:1-14 about Jesus and little children and then how He likens "rescuing" the little child in you to the "rescue" of a lost sheep. Huddle up, of course. Give each other your eyes in a ritual of confidential support and encouragement, then close with blessing prayer. Create the honesty circle that will make it easy for anyone to begin the journey of full disclosure and healing from compulsive behaviors. You are well on your way. Be looking ahead to the conclusion of this sequence of chapters as a basis for your meetings and locate additional resources from the Bibliography at the end of the book.

CHAPTER NINE

CELEBRATION: MY PLACE IN FULL SPECTRUM MASCULINITY

The good news is that millions of men are mending today. They are those who have faced their twisted instincts to be competing, controlling tournament bucks, or systematic hoarders of money and women. They have recognized the symptoms of self-protection and power mongering, and have intentionally cut the nerve of those destructive instincts.

SOME HEALTHY MEN ON PARADE

I watched Bill's tears flow on his wedding day. The assembled family and host of friends thought the uncontrolled tears signaled his deep feelings for his bride. But the three of us at the center aisle knew they were his final release of shame and guilt. Carol had, indeed, forgiven him for wasting his intimacy during high school and college years. I had said to his fiancée during an emergency session six months before, "Carol, you are a lucky woman. Only an absolutely honest man would tell you the whole truth about his high school and college sexual escapades. Look at the risk he took in opening his entire life to you—to let you really know him. You could have rejected him because of his honesty with you, and he was willing to run that risk to build your relationship on complete integrity. But look at how painful the episode was when the two of you sobbed for more than an hour in dealing with his losses. This is a man who is immunized against being unfaithful to you—there has been too much pain involved in confessing the truth. But if you hold the knowledge wrapped in resentment, it is you, not Bill, who is most vulnerable to an extramarital affair—as a way of getting back at him."

Or take Kyle and Karen. "I was a virgin, at least technically, on our wedding day," Kyle reflected. "But I had lied to Karen. She was curious about past sexual contacts I might have had, and I took pride in my having never taken anybody to bed. But I hid the awesome battle I had with my own sexual energy. I wish I could have told her the truth about how humiliating it has been, and how I programmed myself into masturbation as the price paid to keep my virginity. Now, ten years into our marriage, I have finally opened up those adolescent years of frustration and shame. I wasn't vulnerable enough before, I guess."

Randy slipped into the gay community right out of high school. As he was "coming home" he reflected with five of us who continued to hang on while he was away. "I needed friends, mostly, and somebody to take me seriously. Most guys I grew up with were so crazy, so rough, and superficial that I felt really alone. But in the homosexual community I found that people took time to talk to me. As you know, I was into the arts and creative writing. I was never more surprised than to find that I wasn't alone among them. But growing up, I always felt that my music and my writing and my literary tastes set me apart as a misfit. Why didn't anybody back home help me connect my own gifts with Jesus' kind of masculinity? Do you think I can come back?"

Then there are cases more like Rolf and his wife Jerry."We are having an opportunity to see the pattern of God's grace," Rolf explained. "Jerry and I were married ten years ago. I had been a fast-lane fraternity house brat during university days, and she was devastated by her father-loss and by sexual abuse by relatives as a child. At sixteen she gave up a baby for adoption, then followed with a couple of abortions before Jesus stabilized her as an adult. So we married knowing adoption was our only route—the last abortion cost her her uterus.[1]

"I was never able to fault Jerry for her wild and crazy years. I had left my own tracks, and I couldn't accept God's forgiveness for me if I had held Jerry's behavior over her head. We have two adopted sons now, and every day is another miracle for us."

These protected profiles of people I have known well, all of whom will always be important in my network of treasured friends, paint the alternatives in ways that theory rarely does. Integrity comes at an enormous price of courage and risk. But self-protection is quickly and effectively fatal. There are no cheap roads to a meaningful life. It has always been that way.

IMAGES FROM LONG AGO AND FAR AWAY
Noah preached righteousness for 400 years, yet there is no record of his oratory. What he did was to "live integrity," I suppose. And in the low-water mark of decadence in human antiquity, his integrity fell like a mantel of protection over his family. "Just as it was in the days of Noah" (Luke 17:26) becomes the description of conditions which will mark the end of human history. So, salute Noah as a man whose family was stabilized in the worst of times.

Joseph, favorite son in a dysfunctional polygynous family, suffered the humiliation of being sold into slavery by competitive and hateful brothers. How did Joseph survive in the crucible of that abuse? Was it his naivete, or was it his attachment to his parents and his God which stabilized him in Egyptian slavery? His transparent goodness won him early trust, only to be undercut by a scheming Egyptian woman who wanted his body, and when spurned, punished him by falsely accusing him of attempted rape. But with his integrity and vulnerability to people intact, Joseph became a source of hope and truth even in prison.

Released and rising in authority, Joseph spared Egypt a tragic starvation in famine, and brokered scarce food to neighboring Israeli families. Among them he found his own brothers, eventually disclosing himself to them in an episode tinctured with their terror and bathed in his tears and loud wailing. Reunited with his father, Joseph watched as Jacob blessed his sons in a final benediction which bridged the generations—grandfather to grandsons.

Moses was marked for the ultimate abuse: infanticide. Yet his family made the choice of life for him and risked their own death in the process. Found by Pharaoh's daughter and reared in the Egyptian palace by the royal family, he became the national "father figure," leading the Israeli slaves out and on their way to freedom. At the low point in his political life, Moses found shelter and emotional stability in the home of a family whose daughter, Ketura, he would later marry. And his leadership team during the Exodus consisted of his brother, Aaron, and his sister, Miriam.

Consider another Joseph centuries later. He was "betrothed" to Mary, and finding her pregnant during the betrothal and knowing it was not his baby, made a typical "justice-based, left-brained" decision. "Because Joseph her husband was a rightous man ... he had in mind to divorce her quietly" (Matt. 1:20-21).

But God spoke to Joseph through angelic dreams (notice the right-brain appeal!) and eased his fears. Joseph was slowly healed of his insecurity and found his shame fading. At last, he went to retrieve Mary, who seems to have run away as many pregnant teenage girls tend to do. The heavenly messenger had said, "Do not be afraid to take Mary home as your wife, because what is conceived in her is from the Holy Spirit. She will give birth to a son, and you are to give Him the name Jesus, because He will save His people from their sins" (Matt. 1:20-21).

After still another right-brained message in God's "bypass" following Jesus' birth, Joseph escaped with his family into Egypt. With yet another "image" message, Joseph brought them home to Nazareth.

So Joseph not only provided the name Jesus, but furnished the legal registry for His permanent genealogy. You can read it in Matthew's first chapter. But equally important, Joseph gave Jesus the care and nurture that only a father can give a boy, so that Jesus grew up in healthy maturity: in wisdom, in physique, and in healthy relationships with God and others.

Then, finally, at the apex of His teaching ministry, Jesus returned the compliment to Joseph. As he was teaching the disciples to pray, Jesus gave God a new name. The sovereign Elohim, Yahweh-Jehovah, El Shaddai, and Adonai names became, on Jesus' lips, "Our Father"! On another occasion Jesus even used "Daddy, Father,"—"Abba," in which you can almost hear the near universal "Papa"—the first spontaneous syllables of every child in every culture—the redundant "Da-da" and "Pa-pa." And where do you think Jesus learned the meaning of those sound bytes?

JOIN THE "REAL MEN" CLUB!
A new fraternity is forming all over the world. Already you can being to identify some of the members. They are men who are being transformed from one degree of powerful gentleness to another, and this comes directly from God's grace. They are assertive, but unconditionally controlled by respect for the value of people. They are tough-minded, but full of tenderness in their relationships.

The Old Testament canon closes with a description of the forming of a new breed of man. There is a single "marker," a solitary characteristic of these rehabilitated men. You can spot one in an instant. The test criterion is named here in the final words of the Book of Malachi: "See, I will send you the prophet Elijah before that great and dreadful day of the Lord comes. He will turn the hearts of the fathers to their children, and the hearts of the children to their fathers" (Mal. 4:5-6). So the call is clear: The real "survivalists" will be the rough but tender fathers who are devoted to the nurture and care of their children, and their transformation will be in response to the call of Elijah. "When Elijah comes" represents the undying hope that justice and truth will one day control the world.

Those of us who link the Old Testament with the New trace the connection through Elijah. Because when he finally comes, Elijah turns out to be John the Baptist—that tough and gentle final prophet. Zechariah receives the clear prophetic word from an angel:

> He will be a joy and delight to you, and many will rejoice because of his birth, for he will be great in the sight of the Lord. He is never to take wine or other fermented drink, and he will be filled with the Holy Spirit even from birth. Many of the people of Israel will he bring back to the Lord their God. And he will go on before the Lord, in the spirit and power of Elijah, to turn the hearts of the fathers to their children and the disobedient to the wisdom of the righteous—to make ready a people prepared for the Lord (Luke 1:14-17).

This outdoorsman, complete with a stress camper's diet and hooked deep into the masculine spirit, sanctified men's hearts, turning them into effective and affectionate fathers, shutting down their "idols" of work, consumption, and obscenity by sanctifying their male energy into the service of what is good, true, holy, and constructive.

Then to complete the profile of membership in the "Real Men" Club, Jesus comments both on John the Baptist and on the roles of toughness, aggressiveness, even "violence" required for healthy males:

> Jesus began to speak to the people about John: "What was the spectacle that drew you to the wilderness? A reed-bed swept by the wind? (Denoting ambivalence, wishy-washiness.) No? Then what did you go out to see? A man dressed in silks and satins? (Denoting the soft, effeminate career and Peter Pan types.) Surely you must look in places for that. But why did you go out? To see a prophet? (Denoting one who predicts the future.) Yes, indeed, and far more than a prophet. He is the man of whom Scripture says, 'Here is My herald, whom I send on ahead of You, and he will

prepare Your way before You.' I tell you this: Never has there appeared on earth a mother's son greater than John the Baptist, and yet the least in the kingdom of heaven is greater than he.

Ever since the coming of John the Baptist, the kingdom of heaven has been subjected to violence and violent men are seizing it. (Literally, taking it by violence.) For all the prophets and the Law foretold things to come until John appeared, and John is the destined Elijah, if you will but accept it. If you have ears, then hear" (Matt. 11;7-15, NEB).

Luke captures the "violence" sense a little differently:

The Law and the Prophets were proclaimed until John. Since that time, the good news of the kingdom of God is being preached, and everyone is forcing his way into it (Luke 16:16, my translation).

The imagery is pretty troublesome to our "silk and satin" view of feminized religion. The text uses John the Baptist— the "Elijah" messenger—as the focal point of violence: His announcing Jesus produced a violent response among those who rejected the call to integrity, obedience, repentance, and turning from wicked, deceitful, and indulgent living. Then, the silk and satin crowd was left standing in the dust as the "violent" sinners of all sorts took Jesus seriously and stormed into repentance and repudiation of their past wickedness. These storm troops were the unwashed rabble who grabbed on to Jesus' words and took Him seriously.

It is clear why many men have little to do with "silk and satin" churches today. They have to park their masculinity at the door, and nothing "violent" has been announced or grasped in many congregations for generations. And when a man has a clear built-in altimeter which gives him a reading on issues of truth and justice, you can understand why he cannot tolerate a wishy-washy religious environment. Is there no truth to stick by? Is any road as good as another to find your way to heaven? To hell? If so, then most men will say, "Forget it!" and they'll go fishing.

But give a man permission to tap into his considerable sense of justice, his grasp of what is true, and his need for making a muscular and visceral response, and watch out. The real men are ready for action.

TOUGH AND TENDER?

If Elijah and John the Baptist are our backpacker versions of godly manhood, the other end of the spectrum is well represented in Jesus and in Gospels.

Richard Rohr has forced us to look at "two Johns"—the Baptizer and the Apostle. Together they provide the polar extremes between which full spectrum masculinity is vibrant in God's ideal kingdom.[2] John the Baptist is the assertive and straight-shooting risk taker. John the Apostle, according to his own Gospel, saw himself as the one whom Jesus loved. He and his brother James may have been "Sons of Thunder" in some genealogical record, but John the Apostle is our prototype of the artist, the one who caught Jesus in one-on-one intimate encounters of a saving kind. The Fourth Gospel captures more than the other three the pictures of Jesus engaged in private conversations with all sorts of folks.

While Bruce Barton made an important correction to our picture of Jesus "meek and mild" in his best-seller, *The Man Nobody Knows,*[3] Jesus remains our "full spectrum" final Adam, no texture of manhood missing from God's portrait of Himself in His Son. If we find ourselves ignited to masculinity affirmations by watching Him with His whip of leather working over the parasitic money changers in the temple, then we have to drop back in awe as He teaches us how to listen, how to talk about anything of any importance to anyone. Then, in the final showdown with human violence, He turned totally nonviolent, submitting to inhuman abuse and death. After He is strung up to die, even His resurrection is so toned down that most everybody missed it. Instead He began slipping in on the disciples where they were, in the grip of fear and terror. He spoke words of "Peace!" repeatedly to them and "they were overjoyed when they saw the Lord."

So bring every kind of gifted man to Jesus. Whether he is the artistic, gentler, and kinder man, like the Apostle John, or the outspoken man of action like John the Baptist, or any possible mix of those two poles, know that Jesus will connect with their deep manhood. Jesus will bless their masculinity anywhere across the enormous spectrum these two Johns represent.

NO MEMBERSHIP CARD NEEDED

Welcome to the club of men under continuing lifelong construction—men who are being made whole, complete, effective, and blessed. Accept the legitimacy of your personal gifts. Embrace the destiny of being a responsible manager of your sexual energy, letting it fuel your intimacy, your parenting, your productivity, your "expansiveness," and your creativity. Let integrity, courage, and gentleness be your middle names. The future belongs to you, and with your surging energy, you will take it forcefully and with dignity.

 Do-It-Yourself Tips

Take the "full spectrum masculinity test" from John the Baptist to John the Apostle. Where do you land on the spectrum? Are you susceptible to depression when things go bad for you, as John the Baptist was while in prison? Or are you indestructible, up-to-date with your really important life issues, ready to level, to confide in a network of three or four—to let people really know you, as the Apostle John seems to have done?

Reread the John the Baptist descriptions in Matthew 11:7-15 if you resonate with the red-blooded "tell-it-like-it-is" Baptizer. Or read John 21 to track the intimate friendship the Apostle John enjoyed with Jesus if you score higher on the affectional and intimacy scale in your needs for friendships.

Contractor's Crew Notes

Choose your "model of masculinity" from the biblical characters ranging from Noah to the Apostle John. If anybody hasn't read the chapter, run vignettes past the group as a refresher with this instruction: Choose your own biblical "mentor model" from these or others you may want to describe, and tell us why your choice of Bible character nurtures your growing masculinity.

Pick up swatches of John the Baptist and Apostle John Scripture narratives to wrap your session before your prayer huddle. As you continue your "crew sessions," consider looking at additional resources. See the Bibliography beginning on the next page.

BIBLIOGRAPHY OF
MEN'S RESOURCES

Men's Discipleship Development

Bruce Barton, *The Man Nobody Knows*. Bobbs Merrill, 1925; charter edition, 1962.

This surprising best-seller of several generations focuses on the masculine version of the Gospel, takes Jesus out of the soft, effeminate pictures of gowns and uncalloused hands. Barton wrote the book as an adult who was angered at the "gentle Jesus, meek and mild" distortions he had been handed as a boy in Sunday School. We read it to our two sons when they hit junior high school years, morning after morning offered with their cereal in a disguised "family altar" celebration of their emerging manhood.

Verne Becker, *The Real Man Inside: How Men Can Recover Their Identity and Why Women Can't Help*. Grand Rapids: Zondervan, 1992.

Becker's bold and empowering story of his own wasted marriage and half-a-life is the story repeated millions-fold in the cities and villages of Western culture. His appeal for men to meet in groups for intentional agendas of honesty and integrity is another wake-up call of hope to millions of good men who have been turned off by the flamboyance of the popularized versions of the men's movement. This is a call for radical Christian discipleship in which men, thank you, have to "do their own work" with the encouragement of families and children.

Clint and Mary Beckwith, *Time Out! A Men's Devotional*. Ventura, California: Evergreen Communications, Inc., 1989.

Men who keep their devotional lives in ship shape will want to add this to their permanent repertoire. Dozens of top-flight, well-known Christian authors are excerpted by the Beckwiths who offer several other devotional collections too.

Gordon Dalbey, *Father and Son: The Wound, the Healing, the Call to Manhood.* Nashville: Thomas Nelson Publishers, 1992.

Dalbey's thesis is that all men have been wounded by their fathers, since the father is an imperfect representation of God to children. All of us need restoration if we are to be whole men. God is the only perfect Father for the task. Jesus meets us in our woundedness and heals our "father wounds."

Gordon Dalbey, *Healing the Masculine Soul: An Affirming Message for Men and the Women Who Love Them.* Dallas: Word, Inc., 1988.

"Our problem as men is not that we have failed to bond with our women, but rather with our own manly selves." Dalbey invites men to step up to first-quality roles as lover, worker, father, warrior, and godly church member.

Gene Edwards, *A Tale of Three Kings: A Study in Brokenness.* Auburn, Maine: Christian Books, 1980.

David is Saul's "spear catcher," refusing to indulge in the violence that Saul had stooped to in his insecurity and fear of David's gifts and popularity with the people. Then watch Absalom—the third of the kings Edwards treats. This is ideal for reading aloud in small pieces in your "Contractor's Crew" huddles or your E-Team meetings. Or read it for pure poetic enjoyment. Edwards takes the liberties of a poet and represents only selected features of David, his favorite character, sparing us from the dark side of David's intoxication with power, his adultery, murder, and polygamy.

Gene A. Getz, *The Measure of a Man.* Ventura, California: Regal Books, 1974.

Getz offers a brief but helpful outline of highest male aspirations by unpacking the list of Scripture credentials for manhood cited by the Apostle Paul in 1 Timothy 3:1-7 and Titus 1:5-9.

David Hawkins and Ross A. Tunnell III, *Reclaiming Manhood: A 12-Step Journey to Becoming the Man God Meant You to Be.* Wheaton, Illinois: Victor Books, 1992.

Take the Alcoholics Anonymous Twelve Steps and drive them back to their biblical roots. Then spin out a workbook and group agenda guide for "men under construction." You've got *Reclaiming Manhood.* Especially useful for any group of men who can meet regularly to focus on compulsive behavior and support each other in the journey for healing and day-by-day recovery.

Donald Joy, *Becoming a Man: A Celebration of Sexuality, Responsibility, and the Christian Young Man.* Ventura, California: Regal Books, 1990.

I wrote this one for my three grandsons as they plunged into the teenage years. Jason, now eighteen, read every chapter and gave me written notes that changed and shaped the book. "What do I know now at sixty that I wish I had known at sixteen?" motivated the book. "How can I tell Jason, Jordan, and Justin without blowing them away?" controlled and restrained my writing.

Donald Joy, *Unfinished Business: How a Man Can Make Peace with His Past.* Wheaton, Illinois: Victor Books, 1989.

This "original edition" of *Men Under Construction* included expanded chapters and case stories of men in process of coming to integrity and productivity. The hardback edition is still available from the author, as is the audio version in limited quantities for study and for collectors.

Steven J. Lawson, *Men Who Win: Pursuing the Ultimate Prize.* Colorado Springs, Colorado: NavPress, 1992.

This is the athletic version of manhood played out with 1 Corinthians 9:24 as a centerpiece and motif. It will awaken everything competitive and muscular in the Christian man, urging him to "get out of the RAT race and get into the RIGHT race."

J. Allen Peterson, *For Men Only: The Dynamics of Being a Man and Succeeding at It.* Wheaton, Illinois: Tyndale House, 1972.

Forty-plus short chapters by top-notch Christian authors make this a solid devotional resource or a curriculum guide for a men's group.

Richard Rohr, *A Man's Approach to God: Four Talks on Male Spirituality.* Cincinnati: St. Anthony Messenger Press, four cassettes, no date.

Pastor of Cincinnati's Roman Catholic New Jerusalem Community Church, Rohr offers the experience of working with young men in Catholic high schools and continuing as their mentoring pastor into their mid-lives. The seminar tapes are casual, informal, yet laced with insights into Scripture, human experience, and Jungian psychology. "The Hero's Journey," "Creators of Life," "The Boy and the Old Man," and "The Grand Father" are supplemented by extensive dialogue with men in the seminar at New Jerusalem.

Dorothy L. Sayers, *The Man Born to Be King: The Life of Christ in Twelve Dramatic Episodes.* New York: Harper and Row, 1943.

The characters from the Gospels absolutely "live" in the Sayers' radio plays, produced and broadcast over BBC. The images of masculinity are powerful and explicit. We read these plays after breakfast with our two young sons through the high school years with amazing and powerful effects.

David Stoop and Steve Arterburn, *The Angry Man.* Dallas: Word, Inc., 1991.

See your own anger episodes chapter after chapter. Take the ten or so tests the authors share from their counseling practice with families. Missing: any report at all on brain differences which block "putting it into words" when men bottle up emotion. But any man who blows his top or acts irresponsible in traffic will do himself a favor to check these chapters and agendas.

Walter Trobisch, *All a Man Can Be and What a Woman Should Know.* Downers Grove, Illinois: InterVarsity Press, 1983.

Ingrid Trobisch found this manuscript, almost completed, when the famous father, missionary, and author died. She and a son put together the final section in a format which sweeps the suffering man, the reacting man, and the free man. Trobisch playfully suggested this book under a title to match Ingrid's *The Joy of Being a Woman* in counterpoint, *The Pain of Being a Man*. But the book is tender, gentle, and tough of spirit—just like the Walter Trobisch you met in *Promises to Peter, My Beautiful Feeling, I Married You,* and *I Loved a Girl.*

Masculinity, Myths, and the Men's Movement

Patrick Arnold, *Wildmen, Warriors, and Kings: Masculine Spirituality and the Bible.* New York: Crossroad Publishing, 1992.

Here is a tour of the Bible through the lens of mythological archetypes— an obvious evangelical response to Robert Moore's recent lead book on mythology. God is portrayed as wildman, warrior, king, and father. The author takes on radical feminism, and makes male archetypes understandable whether you find them helpful or not. If the myths and archetypes bother you and you wonder how they fit with Scripture, consider what they have in common and what stands outside Judeo-Christian history and values. My growing impression is that they may be rooted in pre-literature story-telling and may express universal yearnings and fears that have been addressed specifically and positively in Jesus and all of God's revelation through Holy Scripture and preserved history. You decide.

Robert Bly, *Iron John.* New York: Addison-Wesley, 1990.

Read the appendix first to get the Grimm's Fairy Tale in mind before trying to follow Bly's poetic-artistic commentary on men's frozen emotional wasteland. The fairy tale makes bad use of parents, finally redeeming them in the end. But if you want to get the idea of what a mentor can do for you that a parent cannot do, read *Iron John* and wait two weeks thinking about who empowered "the boy with the golden hair." Ask yourself who empowered you to embrace your high adult male potential.

Philip Culbertson, *New Adam: The Future of Male Spirituality.* Minneapolis: Augsburg-Fortress, 1992.

Brace yourself for a sweep through the Old Testament, the New Testament, and a critique of the Iron John myth, followed by an alternative set of images in the myth of the White Snake. The David and Jonathan friendship along with Jesus and the Twelve provide important masculinity-defining segments.

Robert L. Moore and Douglas Gillette, *King, Warrior, Magician, Lover.* New York: Harper-Collins, 1990.

Moore and Gillette open up the Jungian foundations of masculine psychology, revealing the shadowy "boy" side of the four archetypes and pointing the way to a renewed sense of self through a mature masculine identity. The authors put forward data from ancient myths and from the Bible's stories (which they sadly reduce to mere myth), throwing modern psychology and culture into the humanistic mix. "King" and "Warrior," for example, become larger than political or military images and denote the self-confidence and self-management within a man—his "king." The "warrior" is a man's driving pattern of productivity—his ability to "complete the task" before going on to meeting personal needs or taking time for meals or pleasure. Moore and Gillette have opened ancient mythology for all of us and have invited a number of responses, among them Patrick Arnold and Philip Culbertson, cited here. See also Moore's earlier release, *Rediscovering Masculine Potentials*, Wilmette, Illinois: Chiron, 1988, four cassette tapes.

Men, Marriage, and Sexuality

George Gilder, *Men and Marriage*. Gretna, Louisiana: Pelican, 1986.

Revised from *Sexual Suicide* in 1973, this secular jaunt through Gilder's "facts of life" about male and female differences interprets the breakdown of monogamy and the usefulness of "eros" in making human societies work. He offers painful critique of militant feminism and the technological "sexual suicide" of which it is a central fixture. See also his *Naked Nomads: Unmarried Men in America*, New York: Quadrangle, 1974. Here Gilder massages the census bureau data to paint a bleak picture of the risk and death rates of single men. Singleness is a high-risk state, risky enough, he reports, that while writing the book he almost became a singles' mortality statistic, caved in, and got married. Secular to the core, it is a chilling piece of "rocks and hills" crying out in print.

Paul Pearsall, *Super Marital Sex: Loving for Life*. New York: Ivy Press, 1987.

Pornography, marital secrets, premarital sex, and preoccupation with sexual orgasm—all come under the gun of Pearsall's conclusions after his clinical work with 500 couples over ten years at Sinai Hospital in Detroit. "Sex is not like tennis," he declares. "Practice does not make perfect. It only leads to more practice." This secular "rocks and hills" book proves that healthy sexual behavior is essential for everybody, not just for Christians.

Research on Men's Development

Ken Druck, *The Secrets Men Keep*. Garden City, New York: Doubleday, 1985.

Druck's "Alive and Male" seminar is here in book form, which means men's group agendas conclude each chapter. For men who are ready to shuck off the burden of their isolation and get real, the author's stories will provide the courage to share secrets with other men. Bring your own biblical and Christian perspectives to enrich the text.

Daniel J. Levinson, *The Seasons of a Man's Life*. New York: Ballantine, 1978.

This is the baseline research on men's mid-life crisis. They have one— every ten years. Read all about it and chart your own "life agendas" at 20,

30, 40, and 50. Most of us are vulnerable to breaking away to new agendas at 17, 27, 37, 47, and we'll likely be restless until 23, 33, 43, and 53. But track your own adventures with his summaries of the "seasons." And share your stories, looking for ways God breaks through to all of us in the journey and past every marker event.

Gail Sheehy, *Passages.* New York: Bantam, 1974.
This is the book which "scooped" Levinson's research and beat him and his team of researchers to press. Popularized and generalized to men's and women's issues, it unpacks the agendas of the life-cycle decades of adult years. See also her very important book on leadership potential, *Pathfinders: Overcoming the Crises of Adult Life and Finding Your Own Path of Well-Being,* New York: William Morrow, 1981.

Carolyn A. Koons and Michael J. Anthony, *Single Adult Passages: Uncharted Territories.* Grand Rapids: Baker Book House, 1991.
Single men and men who are "single again" need this book to find their way in the growing masses of singles in America. The demographics are impressively reported and laid out in diagrams. The book is especially helpful in its interpretation of the complications of divorce and single parenting. "Part Four: Anchoring in Safe Harbors" is especially focused on issues in *Men Under Construction,* with its appeal for the security of a support group for the single man.

Fiction and Images of Masculinity

John Irving, *A Prayer for Owen Meany.* New York: William Morrow, 1989.
This suprising novel built around the life of an undersize, slightly deformed but indestructible kid from the stone quarry social class will connect with any man's feelings of rejection, isolation, and failure. The plot moves through childhood with a few unspeakable episodes of exploitation and abuse, through the high school and college years, and connects with the Vietnam War in a surprising way. You will want to read it and talk about its connections into your own experience.

John Knowles, *A Separate Peace.* New York: Bantam, 1959.
Another classic novel to add to *A Prayer for Owen Meany.* This story set in a male-bonding plot at a boy's private prep school puts your moral core to the test. What goes on between boys? What does loyalty mean? Competition? And why would you come back to the scene to check out the tree where it all centered fifteen years before? It begins with a tiny event involving ordinary boys, then spins out as wide as the universe and as deep as evil itself. This secular piece is a profoundly moral novel. It is worth sharing among adult male friends who are owning their own childhoods and making peace with history.

Walter Wangerin, *The Orphean Passages: The Drama of Faith.* San Francisco: Harper and Row, 1986.
Watch a young boy's faith turn into painful maturity as childhood fears

and the pathos of pastoral ministry continue to forge unshakable Christian perspective and resources. Wangerin is easily the "poet laureate" of Christian fiction. If there is a man who is willing to be in touch with his kinder, gentler self, volunteer to read *Orphean Passages* with him and talk about it.

NOTES

Chapter One. Design: Maleness and Manhood

1. See the notes for Genesis 5 in an NIV Bible. Note the footnote inside the closing quotation mark around "man." It is anybody's guess why the translators did not provide the footnote in Genesis 1, with the first appearance of "man." But "Adam" is "both" male and female—the human species, "the Adam." So we would help ourselves to always read Adam or "man" as "the Adamses." At least then we are ready for all of the plural charges—"Let them have dominion," for example.

2. Frank H. Netter, *The Ciba Collection of Medical Illustrations*, Vol. 2, "A Compilation of Paintings on the Normal and Pathologic Anatomy of the Reproductive System" (New York: Ciba Pharmaceutical Company, 1965). See Section I, Plate 1, "Homologues of Internal Genitalia," and Section I, Plate 2, "Homologues of External Genitalia," pp. 2 and 3, to trace the male-female developmental differentiation in the stages reported in this chapter. For an extended description of these fetal development features see also my *Bonding: Relationships in the Image of God* (Dallas: Word, Inc., 1985), especially chapter 5, "Conception: Differentiating the Adam," pp. 87-107. You can follow the sexual differentiation process by watching the PBS series, *The Body Human: The Sexes,* or you can read about it in M.J. Sherfey, *The Nature and Evolution of Female Sexuality* (New York: Vintage, revised, 1972). If you want to track down a popularized version, including the brain transformation which is described later in this chapter, see Pamela Weintraub, "The Brain: His and Hers," in *Discovery,* April 1981, pp. 15ff.

3. The sexual orientation issue in relation to defective male fetal development is reported in Robert W. Goy and Bruce S. McEwen, *Sexual Differentiation in the Brain,* (Cambridge, Mass.: MIT Press, 1980), especially in the subsection, "Is There an Endocrine Basis for Homosexuality Among Human Males?" pp. 64ff. The medical judgments are that prevention and rehabilitation, along with positive "masculinity support" in the environ-

ment, are the obligations of the family and the medical community. Verifying the power of positive male brain development to compensate for overwhelming negative environmental damage is the astonishing report on the Dominican third-world "laboratory" in which thirty-eight mutant defect males were discovered who began life with complete female external genitalia. The group, spanning four generations and twenty-three interrelated families, was studied beginning in 1972. By a fluke in timing (the 5a-Reductase Factor), although their ovaries were modified internally and were functioning as testicles and the brain was fully masculinized, the testicles remained inside the body. These "girls" were actually thinking like boys, even though the penis development and the dropping of the testicles did not occur until the onset of pubescence. So in a culture in which young boys remained naked until pubescence and young girls wore panties and the only bathing place was the open river, these "boys" were programmed to have sexual orientation appropriate to their rearing and public "identity." Yet of the twenty-five surviving, of which nineteen have been studied in detail, seventeen are living as normal males in culturally sanctioned marriages. One is a rural bachelor living as a male. One cohabits with a woman as a male, but presents himself publicly as a woman. So the "environment" versus "physiological" basis for sexual orientation has given us new concerns about physiology. The environment of the Dominican Republic males, however, was powerfully clear on sexual differentiation and sex-appropriate behavior. The seventeen males who married did so at an average of one year later than their non-defective male peers. In a culture which gives mixed signals or even "mocks" its young boys' interest in girls, and subjects its adolescents to confusing, ambiguous, and politically attractive forms of rebellion to assert independence of family and traditional cultural values, an actual magnet might be made of sexual inversion. You can read about the Dominican discovery in the chief researcher's own words in Julianne Imperato-McGinley, "Androgens and the Evolution of Male-Gender Identity Among Male Pseudohermaphrodites with 5a-Reductase Deficiency" in the *New England Journal of Medicine*, May 31, 1979, pp. 1233ff.

4. See Diane McGuinness, "How Schools Discriminate Against Boys," in *Human Nature*, February, 1979, pp. 82-88.

Chapter Two. Deformity: Father to Son?

1. Thomas Parish and J. Dostal, "Relationships Between Evaluations of Self and Parents by Children from Intact and Divorced Families," in the *Journal of Psychology*, 1980, Vol. 104, pp. 35-38. See also Parish's many other research reports, including, "Evaluations of Self and Parent Figures by Children from Intact, Divorced and Reconstituted Families," *Journal of Youth and Adolescence*, 1980, Vol. 19, pp. 347-51, and "The Impact of Divorce and Subsequent Father Absence on Children's and Adolescents' Self-Concepts" with James C. Taylor, *Journal of Youth and Adolescence*, Vol. 8, 1979, pp. 427-32.

2. George Gilder, *Men and Marriage*, revised and expanded from *Sexual Suicides* (Gretna, La.: Pelican, 1986), p. 6.

3. Arthur Miller, *Death of a Salesman* (New York: Viking Press, 1950), from pp. 118-21.

4. Dan Kiley, *The Peter Pan Syndrome* (New York: Dodd & Mead, 1983).

5. Kenneth Druck, *The Secrets Men Keep: Breaking the Silence Barrier* (Garden City, N.Y.: Doubleday and Co., 1985).

Chapter Three. Default: Hi Mom!

1. See Rebecca Cann, et al., "Mitochondrial DNA and Human Evolution." *Nature*, Vol. 325, Jan. 1, 1987, pp. 31ff, as well as "Out of the Garden of Eden," p. 13, same issue. Consider too *Time*, Jan. 26, 1987, "Everyone's Genealogical Mother," p. 66, and the PBS video special, "Children of Eve," Jan. 27, 1987.

2. See "'Head': Another Name for Husbands," and "'Body': Another Name for Wives" in the book Robbie joined me in designing and writing, *Lovers: What Ever Happened to Eden?* (Dallas: Word, 1987). If we do not shift our paradigm of "bachelor Adam" to the Two Adams, split male and female in Eden and at the Cross, we will continue to miss the integrity intimacy we all long for: "bone of my bone and flesh of my flesh — one flesh naked and unashamed."

3. For Myers-Briggs basic interpretation see Isabel Briggs Myers, *Introduction to Type*, and *Gifts Differing* (Palo Alto, Calif.: Consulting Psychologists Press, 1980, both publications). See David Kiersey and Marilyn Bates, *Please Understand Me* (Del Mar, Calif.: Prometheus Nemesis, 1978), p. 20, for the male/female divergence on the "Thinking-Feeling" spectrum.

4. Carol Gilligan, colleague of Lawrence Kohlberg during his final years at Harvard's Center for the Study of Moral Development, challenged his research done exclusively with males. Her continuing study of women and girls is further helping us to appreciate the "image of God" at the female end of the spectrum. See her *In a Different Voice: Psychological Theory and Woman's Development*, as well as her study of young girls, *Making Connections: The Relational Worlds of Adolescent Girls* (Cambridge, Mass.: Harvard University Press, 1982 and 1990).

5. My baseline on "adolescence" appeared in "Adolescents in Socio-Psychological Perspective" in Roy B. Zuck and Warren S. Benson, *Youth Education in the Church*, Chicago: Moody Press, 1968, rev. 1978). Then, after working with the Department of Health and Human Services' Office of Adolescent Pregnancy Prevention, I struck again in *Parents, Kids, and Sexual Integrity* (Dallas, Word, 1988). There I further define the cultural invention of adolescence and invite Christians to break with the culture in empowering our young without their turning to peers to initiate them with destructive rituals. Now, I am ready to complete a cross-cultural comparison in my new *Empower Your Kids! Alternatives to Adolescence* which will be ready in 1993.

6. Sheldon and Eleanor Glueck, *Unraveling Juvenile Delinquency* (Cambridge, Mass.: Harvard University Press, 1950). For the data on the New York City Youth Board experiment, see Maude M. Craig and Selma J. Glick, *A Manual of Procedures for Application of the Glueck Prediction Table* (New York: Youth Board Research Institute of New York, 1965).

7. Ken Magid and Carol McKelvey, *High Risk* (New York: Bantam, 1987).

8. Herman Hesse, *Narcissus and Goldmund,* tr. by Ursule Molinaro (New York: Farrar, Straus and Giroux, 1968).

Chapter Four. Disorientation: In Search of Self?

1. See my *Becoming a Man: Sex, Strength, and the Secrets of Becoming a Man* (Ventura, Calif.: Regal Books, 1990).

2. See also my *Celebrating the New Woman in the Family,* my gift to three teenage granddaughters (Lexington, Ky.: Bristol House, Ltd., 1993).

3. Ken Magid, *High Risk,* pp. 71ff.

4. Paul Tournier, *Secrets* (Richmond, Va.: John Knox Press, 1965).

5. Harry Harlow, *Speaking of Love Theory and Therapy,* a two-cassette tape series on his career-long study of rhesus monkeys (New York: McGraw-Hill, 1974).

6. See the Frank Netter citation from chapter 1 notes.

Chapter Five. Bonding: Who Could Love Me as I Am?

1. Mike Mason has given us a classic, worth reading aloud for the sheer simple power of his words, *The Mystery of Marriage: As Iron Sharpens Iron,* complete with a guest foreword by Professor J.I. Packer (Portland, Ore.: Multnomah Press, 1985).

2. C.S. Lewis, "As the Ruin Falls," in *Poems* (New York: Harcourt Brace Jovanovich, Inc., 1964), pp. 109-10.

3. Paul Pearsall, *Super Marital Sex: Loving for Life* (New York: Ballantine, 1987), p. 71.

4. See my chapters, "Pair Bonding: What God Joins Together," and "What Has Gone Wrong with the Bonding?" in my *Bonding: Relationships in the Image of God* (Dallas: Word, Inc., 1985), pp. 33-86.

5. Find my *Re-Bonding: Preventing and Restoring Damaged Relationships* (Dallas: Word, 1986).

Chapter Six. Competing: Scoring and Other Rewards

1. Wilt Chamberlain's latest memoir is entitled, *A View from Above* (New York: Random House, 1991).

2. Melvin Konner defines "tournament species" in *The Tangled Wing: Biological Constraints on the Human Spirit* (New York: Holt, Rinehart & Winston, 1982), pp. 276ff. The characteristic of males in tournament species is remarkably like the competitive macho human male I'm describing in this chapter. Contrast the species behaviors with those of species which practice exclusive, monogamous pair bonding for a chilling comparison of people you know.

3. See our *Lovers: What Ever Happened to Eden?* (Dallas: Word, Inc., 1987) for a book devoted to exploring the entire Judeo-Christian biblical material dealing with men and women and their roles and relationships.

Chapter Eight. Meltdown: Recovering Security

1. Larry Crabb, *Inside Out* (Colorado Springs, Colo.: NavPress, 1988). Among all of Dr. Crabb's many books, this one stands apart in its profound and courageous representation of God's ways of bringing complete inner healing.

2. Patrick Carnes, in his *Out of the Shadows: Understanding Sexual Addiction* (Minneapolis: CompCare, 1983), p. 137, offers an adaptation of the well-known "Twelve Steps" of Alcoholics Anonymous. I have made a further adaptation to identify more explicitly the distinctly Christian and Wesley-based resources which more powerfully undergird rehabilitation from sexual addiction and other compulsive-damaged patterns of living.

3. I am indebted here to my colleague Dr. Mike Henderson whose doctoral dissertation at our mutual alma mater, Indiana University, explored John Wesley's various "structures" in the movement which has been cited for "saving a nation." To locate the dissertation, look for David Michael Henderson, "John Wesley's Instructional Groups,"unpublished dissertation at Bloomington, Ind.: Indiana University, 1980. I have summarized relevant parts of his Appendix B citation of "Orders of a Religious Society Meeting in Fetter Lane" which are found in J.S. Simon, *John Wesley and the Religious Societies* (London: Epworth Press, 1952), pp. 196-98. Henderson's description of the Penitent Bands, the Bands, the Class Meeting, and the Societies is the focus of the entire dissertation. My great-grandfather, W.W. Hulet, was a church-planting evangelist and open-air preacher. He also was a close associate of Vivian Dake, founder of the "Pentecost Bands" and "Missionary Bands" in the Free Methodist Church as it moved west soon after 1860 from Pekin, New York and St. Charles, Illinois, its twin points of origin. The frontier version of Free Methodism was too energetic, too effective for the comfort of the Eastern church, and the work of Vivian Dake and others from whom my genes and my vision seem to have descended was largely ignored and opposed at the national level. Carrie Dake Kline, whose sons Frank and Bruce have blessed the world in my generation, was named for my Grandmother Carrie Hulet Joy. The Dakes visited the Hulet home in Kansas and Kansas City and evidently admired the young daughter of W.W. and Minnie Hulet.

Chapter Nine. Celebration: My Place in Full Spectrum Masculinity

1. For a dozen cases, including this one retold, see the medical, gynecological, and moral-spiritual reflection I share with Dr. David Hager to whom I frequently refer couples for obstetrical and gynecological attention. See *Women at Risk: The Real STD Story* (Lexington, Ky.: Bristol Books, Ltd., 1993).

2. Richard Rohr, *A Man's Approach to God: Four Talks on Male Spirituality* (Cincinnati: St. Anthony Messenger Press, n.d.). Listen to Tape One, "The Hero's Journey," in which he puts the "two Johns" forward as contrasting stages in a man's development. I separate from his understandings for two reasons: (1) Both the gentler, love-motivated Apostle John and the

rigorous, justice-righteousness preoccupied outdoorsman John the Baptist hold open abundant space between them for the rest of us to find freedom in sanctifying our uniqueness and our masculinity and male identity. Also (2) I am impressed that "developmentally" John the Baptist appears earlier than the more seasoned, gentler Apostle John. If you continue in the tape series, Pastor Rohr modifies his thesis in the discussion on Tape Three, "The Boy and the Old Man."

3. See the classic biography of Jesus in Bruce Barton's correction to the effeminate stereotypes of his Sunday School artwork. This Madison Avenue advertising man, moved by a motive to set the record straight about Jesus, wrote *The Man Nobody Knows* (Bobbs Merrill, 1925 and dozens of printings since. A charter edition was released in 1962).

INDEX